shaken

250 classic cocktails with a twist

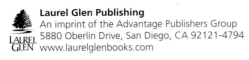

Laurel Glen Publishing
An imprint of the Advantage Publishers Group
5880 Oberlin Drive, San Diego, CA 92121-4794
www.laurelglenbooks.com

All notations of errors or omissions should be addressed to Laurel Glen Publishing, Editorial Department, at the above address. All other correspondence (author inquiries, permissions, and rights) concerning the content of this book should be addressed to Murdoch Books, Pier 8/9, 23 Hickson Road, Millers Point NSW 2000, Australia.

NOTE: Those who might be at risk from the effects of salmonella poisoning (the elderly, pregnant women, young children, and those with a compromised immune system) should consult their physician before trying recipes made with raw eggs.

ISBN 1-59223-341-4
Library of Congress Cataloging-in-Publication Data available upon request.

Printed in China by Toppan Printing
1 2 3 4 5 09 08 07 06 05

Chief Executive: Juliet Rogers
Publisher: Kay Scarlett
Concept and art direction: Marylouise Brammer
Project manager: Zoë Harpham
Photographer: Tim Robinson
Creative consultant and stylist: Marcus Hay
Recipes by: Jeremy Shipley, Jane Lawson, and the Murdoch Books test kitchen
Recipe introductions by: Francesca Newby and Katri Hilden
Text editor and introductory text: Katri Hilden
Designer: Annette Fitzgerald
US editor: Justine Harding
Drinks consultant and preparation: Jeremy Shipley
Editorial Director: Diana Hill
Production: Monika Paratore
Stylist's assistants: Tamara Boon, Nicolle Churi, Tanya Laycock, and Jenny Vidler

The publishers and stylist would like to thank the following for supplying furniture, props, antiques, and kitchenware: Alex Liddy, Blake Watson European Furniture and Restoration, Breville Pty Ltd, Caravan Interiors, David Edmonds, Design Mode International, Dinosaur Designs, FY2K, Gallery in Toto, H.W.I. Harfords Antiques, Homewares, House of Bamboo, Judy Porter Interiors, Jurass, Kalinka, Kosta Boda, Mix(d), Mud Australia, Orient House, Orson & Blake, Pat Farrell (Sculptor), Plenty, Positively Curlewis Street, Spence & Lyda, Wheel & Barrow, Wild Rhino, The Art of Wine and Food. For fabrics and wallpapers: Brunschwig & Fils, Chee Soon & Fitzgerald, Designers Guild at Arc Homewares, La La Zu, Signature Prints, South Pacific Fabrics. For tiled backgrounds: Bisanna Tiles, Pazotti. For background paints: Porters Paints. For rugs and carpets: Customweave, Designer Rugs. For lighting: Maren Kohlwage. For fashion and clothing: Dinosaur Designs, Flying Standard, Pratten Shoes and Accessories, Tim O'Connor. Special thanks to Jo Neville of Paper Couture for customized cocktail umbrellas, and for the ongoing patience of Helen and David at Signature Prints and Casey and Brian at Chee Soon & Fitzgerald for the seemingly endless borrowing of product to create the inspiring backgrounds. We would also like to thank 42 Below Vodka for supplying alcohol.

shaken

250 classic cocktails with a twist

Jane Lawson

Photography by Tim Robinson
Styling by Marcus Hay

LAUREL
GLEN

San Diego, California

contents

ready, set, shake! Life isn't always a smooth ride, but luckily there's a chill-out lounge called the cocktail bar. To step into the sleek, sexy world of cocktails is to enter a zone of ageless glamour, where the mind unfrazzles, tensions unravel and the senses soak up a multitude of sins. Slip on some sultry music, slide into something slinky, and ponder again that eternal question: shaken or stirred?

notes for the lounge lizard

Cocktails are synonymous with glamour-pusses, urban sophisticates, and the cosmopolitan set. With every single sip, we cannot help but luxuriate in these glittering associations. From their rustic beginnings masking fiery bootleg liquor, cocktails are now on the cusp of a golden age, with spirit producers infusing classic spirits such as gin, vodka, and tequila with exciting new flavors, promising infinite possibilities for those seeking the latest cocktail sensations.

There's no special mystique involved in cocktail making. It is an easy art to master, and with a little dedicated practice, you'll be serving drinks with flair and panache. All you need are a few simple implements, some basic ingredients, a steady hand, a highly developed sense of fun, and imagination.

There's a cocktail in this book to suit any mood or occasion, from the snootiest soirée to splashing poolside frolics, smashing parties, and after-dinner meltdowns. We'll even show you how to infuse spirits and whip up fruit purées for special "signature" cocktails.

Before starting, a few quick words. Our recipes make one cocktail using fresh, ripe fruit and fresh fruit juices unless otherwise specified. And remember that although they may taste innocent, cocktails are highly intoxicating. So if you're hosting a cocktail party, offer plenty of food and nonalcoholic refreshments so your guests will remember what a fabulous time they had!

the bar essentials

You don't need truckloads of fancy implements to create a classy cocktail, and most of them you'll find lurking somewhere in your kitchen.

One implement you'll definitely need to buy if you don't already have one is a cocktail shaker, available in two basic types. A **standard shaker** usually has three stainless steel pieces: a canister that holds the ice, a lid with a built-in strainer that seals tightly over the top, and a twist-off cap. The **Boston shaker** often has a mixing glass as its base, snugly overlapped by a stainless steel top. It doesn't have an built-in strainer, so you'll need a separate strainer to filter the drink during pouring. The most widely used is a **hawthorn strainer**, which has a distinctive circular head with a spring coil that fits around the metal half of a Boston shaker.

The other major implement most budding cocktail stars will need is an **electric blender**. If you're a total fanatic, invest in a heavy-duty model with a powerful motor and sturdy blades that can handle whole ice cubes (check the manufacturer's instructions). If your blender is a little lightweight, you'll need to crush the ice cubes before putting them in the blender. To help your blades last longer, add the liquid ingredients to the blender first, then the ice.

Next, find yourself a large **pitcher** with a pouring spout to use as a mixing glass; this is especially useful for making multiple quantities of mixed drinks. You'll also need **measuring spoons** and a **jigger** for measuring alcohol. Jiggers usually have double-sided cups, one holding $\frac{1}{2}$ or 1 ounce, the other holding $1\frac{1}{2}$ or 2 ounces.

A long-handled bar spoon (preferably stainless steel) is used for stirring cocktails and "floating" ingredients in layered drinks. It can also be used for "muddling" fruit and herbs, or you could buy a special muddler, which is essentially a wooden pestle, from specialty kitchen stores.

Ice, ice, and more ice is essential to a cool cocktail, so you'll need plenty of ice-cube trays, an ice bucket for storing ice cubes, and a pair of tongs or an ice scoop for dispensing ice—never use your hands!

Other handy implements include a citrus squeezer, chopping board, fruit knife, vegetable peeler, and zester. For those finishing touches, stock up on plain and colored toothpicks, pretty cocktail umbrellas, swizzle sticks, and straws of all description.

glass class

Purists will insist on using the right glass for every drink. Short mixed drinks on the rocks are served in an old-fashioned glass or tumbler; long mixed drinks are shaken, stirred, or built in a highball glass or in a slightly deeper collins glass. Cocktails without ice are poured into stemmed glasses to keep hot hands away from the drink. Short drinks such as martinis are served in a triangular cocktail or martini glass. Champagne cocktails and some wine cocktails use a champagne flute, while cocktails containing egg yolks are usually dished out in goblets. Mixed or blended drinks are often served in a tulip-shaped glass. Other glasses include shot glasses, brandy balloons (enormous bowled glasses for swirling, sniffing, and swilling fine brandies), and the sour glass, which resembles a champagne flute but has a shorter stem.

tricks of the trade

Here's a really cool tip for making a really cool cocktail: have everything blisteringly cold. Chill all your ingredients before using, and chill the glasses too—or leave a scoop of ice in them while preparing your drinks. Always use fresh ice for each drink, and buy the best ingredients you can find. Have all ingredients ready to go before you start mixing, shaking, stirring, or building your drinks, and don't overfill shakers or mixers. To avoid spillage, never fill a glass to the brim, and remember to leave room for the garnish. When serving a cocktail, present the glass by its base or stem so you don't put hot, sticky fingerprints all over it. Finally, make each drink to order, as cocktails lose their verve over time. On the following pages are some techniques you'll find handy.

Crushing ice

Firmly wrap some ice cubes in a dry, clean dish towel and gently whack them with a mallet or against a solid bench. Bash up a big batch and stash it in the freezer.

Blending

Purée the cocktail ingredients in a blender to a smooth, drinkable consistency, but don't overblend or you'll have a weak, watery concoction. Unless you have a heavy-duty blender, use crushed ice rather than ice cubes in your blender.

Shaking

Half-fill the cocktail shaker with crushed ice, add the other ingredients, and vertically shake the canister vigorously until the shaker is frosty outside (ten seconds should do, but if your cocktail is very creamy or syrupy, you might need to double the time). Strain into a chilled glass. Carbonated drinks should never be shaken or they'll lose their fizz.

Stirring For sparkling clean looks, certain cocktails are stirred in a mixing glass or pitcher with a handful of ice cubes. This chills the alcohol quickly without diluting it. The cocktail is then strained into a glass.

Floating Gently pour the liqueur or spirit into the glass over the back of a spoon. Add the ingredients in the order specified in the recipe and do not mix—the idea is to create a layered effect.

Muddling Grind, crush, or mash fresh fruit or herbs with sugar (usually in a cocktail shaker), using a muddler or bar spoon to release all the flavors.

Adding egg white Slide an egg white into a small glass receptacle and use a sharp knife to cut or slice away a portion of egg white to slip into your drink.

Snazzy ice cubes Freeze fruit juice in an ice-cube tray, perhaps with some mint leaves or diced fruit.

some classic twists

Many recipes in this book will mention any garnish traditionally used to grace a particular drink. Citrus twists and citrus spirals receive special mention here as they are a favorite little flourish, but with the more outlandish tropical concoctions, let your imagination run wild—use as many skewered fruits, swizzle sticks, and tiny parasols as you like!

Citrus twist Use a citrus peeler or very sharp knife to slice a thin, wide strip of peel from the citrus fruit, avoiding the bitter white pith. Make a small cut across the peel and twist it in opposite directions (do this over the drink to release a fine spray of zesty oils) and serve the twist on the side of the glass or in the drink.

Citrus spiral Use a citrus peeler, zester, or sharp knife to slice a long, continuous strip of peel from the fruit. The longer the peel, the greater the curl.

for a special touch

Many recipes call for **sugar syrup**, which you can buy or make very easily. Simply place equal quantities of water and sugar in a saucepan and stir well to dissolve the sugar. Bring to a boil, reduce the heat, and simmer until reduced by half. Allow to cool, pour into an airtight container, and refrigerate. **Fruit purées** give fruity cocktails that extra lift. All you do is blend fresh fruit with a fruit liqueur, pour it into a two-cup airtight container, seal, and refrigerate. Try these! **Mango** Blend the flesh of 4 ripe mangoes with 2 ounces of mango liqueur. **Peach** Blend 6–8 sliced peaches with 2 ounces of peach liqueur. **Raspberry** Blend 3 cups of raspberries with 2 ounces of raspberry liqueur. **Strawberry** Blend 4 cups of hulled strawberries with 2 ounces of strawberry liqueur.

23

Infused spirits have taken off in a big way. Vodka alone is now available in fantastic flavors like bison grass, vanilla, honey, citrus, peach, black currant, sloe berry, pepper, and chocolate. But why not be your own mix-master and infuse your own potions? Vodka is the perfect starting base, as it is neutral in color and flavor. Use good-quality vodka, start with small batches, and plan ahead: you'll need to steep it for at least three days. The quantities here will infuse a four-cup bottle of vodka, gin, vermouth, or tequila, so adjust the ingredients accordingly. Basil or mint 8–10 basil or mint leaves, wrapped in a thin muslin cloth. Blueberry 15 blueberries. Cinnamon 2 cinnamon sticks. Chili 5 red bird's-eye chilies. Coffee 10–15 whole roasted coffee beans. Lemongrass 1–2 stems.

Lychee 8–10 peeled, seeded lychees—if canned, add 1 ounce lychee syrup. **Peach** 3 sliced peaches. **Raspberry** 15 raspberries. **Strawberry** 6 sliced strawberries. **Vanilla** 2 vanilla beans, sliced down the middle. **Watermelon** 10 nice chunks.

How to do it Pour your chosen spirit into a four-cup airtight or screw-top container (reserve the empty bottle). Add the other ingredients, seal the lid tightly, and store in a dark, cool, dry place for 3–5 days. Gently shake the mixture now and then, and check how the flavor is developing. The longer you leave it, the stronger it will become. If it becomes too strong, dilute it with unflavored spirits until you reach your preferred intensity. When you're done, strain the liquid into the original bottle and store in the freezer, ready to drink.

bubbles Nothing speaks of celebration, exhilaration, excitement, and exaltation quite as eloquently as the popping of a champagne cork and the gentle tinkle of clinking flutes. Champagne cocktails,

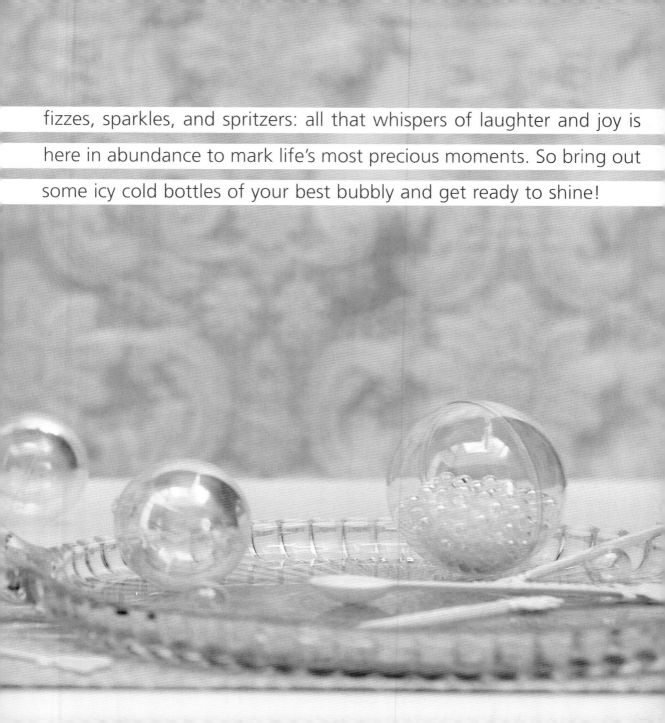

fizzes, sparkles, and spritzers: all that whispers of laughter and joy is here in abundance to mark life's most precious moments. So bring out some icy cold bottles of your best bubbly and get ready to shine!

Life isn't all beer and skittles—some occasions call for a dash of elegance and panache. And what could be more civilized and refined than sipping a **champagne cocktail** while dressed to the nines and practicing the gentle art of conversation in congenial company? The cocktails in this chapter are for **special** times—births, marriages, anniversaries—or whenever life's been a little flat and you need a fast injection of fun or exuberant **decadence**. But first, a point of protocol. Champagne refers to the celebrated liquid produced in the French region of the same name, whose branding is zealously protected. Other **bubblies** made using the same technique are known by the more prosaic moniker of **sparkling wine**, but the end result is arguably equally delightful. Whether you imbibe champagne or sparkling wine, these ambrosial cocktails deserve the best you can afford. And make sure you give your bubblies a really good **chilling** to bring out their luscious bouquet and mouthfeel. The cocktails in this chapter call on heavenly additions such as **brandy**, amaretto, and Grand Marnier; a cornucopia of **liqueurs**—peach, ginger, vanilla, black currant, blackberry, and strawberry, as well as limoncello and blue curaçao—and classic spirits such as Campari, **gin**, and **vodka**. Other bar basics include club soda, sugar syrup, Angostura bitters, and the odd bottle of pinot noir. So now that we've covered the essentials, let's get popping!

Fashions come and fashions go, but the true classic

is untouchable.

classic champagne cocktail

1 sugar cube
Dash of Angostura bitters
1 oz. brandy
Chilled champagne or sparkling wine

Place the sugar cube in a chilled champagne flute. Add the bitters, then
the brandy. Slowly top up with champagne or sparkling wine.

Serve these exquisite berry-laden bubblies on a silver platter in your finest flutes and wait for the accolades to roll in.

champagne berry cocktails

6 sugar cubes
Dash of Angostura bitters
Zest of 1 lime, very finely sliced
2 cups blackberries, raspberries, blueberries, or strawberries
1 bottle of chilled champagne or sparkling wine

Place a cube of sugar in six chilled champagne flutes and add a dash of bitters to each. Divide the lime zest and berries among the flutes and slowly top up with champagne or sparkling wine. Serves 6.

Apples were nothing but trouble for Eve, but a couple of these might just be your ticket to the Garden of Eden.

apple and Calvados champagne cocktail

1/2 oz. Calvados
1/2 oz. clear apple juice
Chilled champagne or sparkling wine

Pour the Calvados and apple juice into a chilled champagne flute, then carefully top up with champagne or sparkling wine.

BARTENDER'S TIP This is one of those rare occasions when fresh isn't best. Freshly squeezed apple juice makes for a cloudy cocktail, so to keep it sparkling, use the bottled variety.

When life goes a little pear-shaped, this sublime nectar will make you feel like a princess again.

poire royale

1/2 oz. Poire William
1/2 oz. peach liqueur
1 teaspoon elderflower cordial
Chilled champagne or sparkling wine
Thin pear slice

Pour the Poire William, peach liqueur, and elderflower cordial into a chilled champagne flute, then slowly top up with champagne or sparkling wine. Garnish with a pear slice.

BARTENDER'S TIP You can buy elderflower cordial or make it at home. Boil 8 1/2 cups water with 4 1/2 cups sugar until the sugar dissolves and the syrup thickens slightly. Pour it onto six elderflower heads in a sterile glass jar and steep overnight. Strain, add lemon juice to taste, and keep refrigerated for a few days. Dilute with water, if necessary.

poire royale

From sun-drenched lemon groves along the sparkling coast of
Naples comes lovely limoncello to make this cocktail shine.

limoncello cocktail

1/3 oz. lime juice
1/2 oz. limoncello
Chilled champagne or sparkling wine

Pour the lime juice and limoncello into a chilled champagne flute, then
slowly top up with champagne or sparkling wine.

As opulent and lavish as the celebrated hotel that shares its name, this drink is all style.

Savoy

½ oz. Campari
½ oz. ruby-red grapefruit juice
½ oz. lychee juice
Chilled champagne or sparkling wine
Orange twist

Pour the Campari, grapefruit juice, and lychee juice into a chilled champagne flute, then slowly top up with champagne or sparkling wine. Garnish with an orange twist.

Sound the trumpets and roll out the carpet. Welcome in the king of drinks to slake the thirst of the blue blood in us all.

kir royale

2 dashes black currant liqueur
Chilled champagne or sparkling wine

Pour the black currant liqueur into a chilled champagne flute and slowly top up with champagne or sparkling wine.

A palace made of gin? Too many of these and you'll be seeing castles in the air and clouds in your coffee.

gin palace

1/2 oz. gin
1/2 oz. blackberry liqueur
1/3 oz. vanilla liqueur
Chilled champagne or sparkling wine
3 blueberries

Pour the gin, blackberry liqueur, and vanilla liqueur into a chilled champagne flute. Slowly top up with champagne or sparkling wine and garnish with blueberries.

Savoy

Make your night a fizz not a fizzle with long, cool, sparkly gin.

gin fizz

Ice cubes
1/2 oz. gin
1/2 oz. lemon juice
1/3 oz. sugar syrup
Club soda
Lemon wedge

Half-fill a cocktail shaker with ice. Add the gin, lemon juice, and sugar syrup, then shake well. Strain into a highball glass half-filled with ice, then top up with club soda. Garnish with a small wedge of lemon.

Putting on the Ritz is a snip with this rosy fizz.

Ritz fizz

1/2 oz. blue curaçao
1/2 oz. amaretto
Dash of lemon juice
Chilled champagne or sparkling wine
Rose petal

Pour the curaçao, amaretto, and lemon juice into a chilled champagne flute and slowly top up with champagne or sparkling wine. Garnish with a floating rose petal.

Pining for a flirty encounter? Find a sexy stranger, flutter those lashes, and sigh languorously as you nibble that cherry.

flirtini

¹/₂ oz. pineapple vodka
¹/₂ oz. pineapple juice
Chilled champagne or sparkling wine
Maraschino cherry

Pour the vodka and pineapple juice into a chilled martini glass. Slowly top up with champagne or sparkling wine and garnish with a maraschino cherry.

BARTENDER'S TIP Many vodka companies are now producing pineapple vodka, but if you can't find it, you can use plain vodka.

This purr-fectly tarty tipple is designed to bring out the sex kitten in you.

ginger puss

Ice cubes
1½ oz. peach-infused vodka (see recipe on page 25)
½ oz. ginger liqueur
1 oz. cranberry juice
⅓ oz. lime juice
Sparkling apple juice

Fill a tall glass three-quarters full with ice. Pour the vodka into the glass, then the ginger liqueur, cranberry juice, and lime juice. Top up with sparkling apple juice and stir well with a bar spoon.

flirtini

Born in 1948 in Harry's Bar and named after an Italian painter, the Bellini tells the secrets of Venice in the summer.

Bellini

1/2 oz. peach liqueur
1 oz. peach juice or nectar
Chilled champagne or sparkling wine

Pour the peach liqueur and peach juice into a chilled champagne flute. Slowly top up with champagne or sparkling wine.

If the original version isn't sinful enough, try this decadent crimson concoction.

scarlet Bellini

1/2 oz. peach liqueur
1 oz. blood-orange juice
Chilled champagne or sparkling wine
Half a blood-orange slice

Pour the peach liqueur and orange juice into a chilled champagne flute. Slowly top up with champagne or sparkling wine. Garnish with half a slice of blood orange.

Mango brings a luscious smile to the mouth and makes the feet inclined to tango.

mango Bellini

½ oz. mango liqueur
½ oz. mango juice
Chilled champagne or sparkling wine

Pour the mango liqueur and mango juice into a chilled champagne flute.
Slowly top up with champagne or sparkling wine.

A vanilla Bellini made beautiful with a spine-tingling surge of strawberry liqueur.

vellini

¹/₂ oz. vanilla vodka
¹/₂ oz. strawberry liqueur
Chilled champagne or sparkling wine

Pour the vodka and strawberry liqueur into a chilled champagne flute. Slowly top up with champagne or sparkling wine.

scarlet Bellini

Adds color to your cheeks and a little sparkle to your step.

cranberry and vodka sparkle

Ice cubes
1/2 cup cranberry juice
1/2 cup lemonade or mineral water
1/3 oz. lime juice
1/2 oz. vodka

Half-fill a mixing pitcher with ice. Pour in the cranberry juice, lemonade or mineral water, lime juice, and vodka. Stir, then pour into a highball glass.

Pucker up for a perky experience that kisses you right back.

blueberry sour

1 tablespoon frozen lemon sorbet
1/2 oz. vodka
Chilled champagne or sparkling wine
6 blueberries

Spoon the sorbet into a chilled martini glass. Pour in the vodka and slowly
top up with champagne or sparkling wine. Garnish with blueberries.

There comes a time in the evening when a lady needs to freshen up.

blackberry spritzer

Ice cubes
1/2 oz. Grand Marnier
1/2 oz. black currant liqueur
1/3 oz. lemon juice
6 blackberries
Club soda

Half-fill a highball glass with ice. Pour in the Grand Marnier, black currant liqueur, and lemon juice. Add the blackberries and top up with club soda.

A fruitful way to take your glass of daily red—just what the good doctor ordered.

pinot sangria spritzers

Ice cubes
1 bottle of pinot noir
1 cup orange juice
1 orange, sliced into half moons
1 lemon, sliced into half moons
1 lime, sliced into half moons
2 cups chilled lemon or lime club soda

Put the ice cubes, pinot noir, and orange juice in a large pitcher and stir well. Add the sliced fruit and leave in the fridge to chill for 30 minutes. Add the club soda and serve in tall glasses, with extra ice if you like. Serves 4–6.

blueberry sour

chic If you feel sweetness is a plague and your wit and palate veer sharply toward the dry side, you might find these elegant cocktails too sexy for words. Oozing style and sophistication, these are drinks for classy, confident types capable of taking the bitter with the sweet. Acerbic, astringent, and invigorating aperitifs mix it with many a dry, wry, macerating martini to sharpen the mind as well as the appetite.

Gin, vodka, and vermouth are the classic culprits behind this searingly smart set of seductive favorites and memorable martinis. Here our vodka takes on some ultra-cool associations, infused with mandarin, bison grass, and sloe berry. Campari makes a strong impression too, with a special guest appearance by its somewhat less bitter Italian cousin aperol. You'll find the odd liqueur from the more exotic end of the flavor spectrum: sweet and sour apple schnapps, lychee liqueur, vanilla liqueur, and the oh-so-continental limoncello. Japanese sake makes a surprise debut, emphasizing the cosmopolitan connections of this highly select company. A major bittersweet contributor to these bracing libations is a full-throttled squeeze of fresh citrus juice, from lemon and lime to blood orange and ruby grapefruit, with cranberry juice offering an equally tart rejoinder. Of course you'll need buckets of ice, as these cocktails must be served arctically cold. And in keeping with our disapproval of ostentatious frippery, we shall also keep our garnishes simple and classy: olives, a twist of lemon or orange, a wedge of lime, the odd maraschino cherry, and a pearl onion or two. Stock up on club soda, check your sugar syrup levels, and maybe even invest in some lime juice cordial, by which we mean the syrupy, thick cordial extracted from real limes—definitely not the impossibly green cordial found on supermarket shelves! Over to you!

Proffer a tray of these and there won't be a dry eye in the house.

dry martini

Ice cubes
1 teaspoon dry vermouth
3 oz. gin
Green olive or a lemon twist

Half-fill a mixing glass with ice. Add the dry vermouth, stir to coat the ice, and then strain out the excess. Add the gin, then stir and strain into a chilled martini glass. Garnish with a green olive or a twist of lemon.

If gin brings a tear to the eye, try the martini's milder cousin.

vodkatini

Ice cubes
1/3 oz. dry vermouth
2 3/4 oz. vodka
Lemon twist

Half-fill a mixing glass with ice. Add the dry vermouth, stir to coat the ice, and then strain out the excess. Add the vodka, then stir and strain into a chilled martini glass. Garnish with a twist of lemon.

The perfect version of the perfect drink promises the perfect start to a perfect evening.

perfect martini

Ice cubes
2 oz. gin
1/2 oz. dry vermouth
1/2 oz. sweet vermouth
Green olives or a lemon twist

Half-fill a mixing glass with ice. Pour in the gin, dry vermouth, and sweet vermouth and stir. Strain into a chilled martini glass and garnish with green olives or a twist of lemon.

Not everyone can handle a searingly dry martini. Here's one for those who appreciate the lusher side of life.

sweet martini

Ice cubes
2¹/₂ oz. gin
¹/₂ oz. sweet red vermouth
Maraschino cherry or an olive

Fill a mixing glass at least two-thirds full of ice. Add the gin and vermouth and stir gently. Strain into a chilled martini glass and garnish with a maraschino cherry or an olive.

perfect martini

You can almost feel sunshine, lollipops, and rainbows in every blessed drop.

lemon drop martini

1/2 oz. sugar syrup
1/2 oz. lemon juice
Ice cubes
2 oz. vodka
Lemon twist

Place the sugar syrup and lemon juice in a cocktail shaker. Stir until the sugar has dissolved, then half-fill the shaker with ice. Add the vodka and shake well. Strain into a chilled martini glass and garnish with a twist of lemon.

When the martini mysteriously fell out of favor,

a little apple schnapps brought it back into flavor.

sour apple martini

Ice cubes
1 1/2 oz. sweet and sour apple schnapps
1 1/2 oz. vodka
1/3 oz. lime juice
Thin apple slice
Lime spirals

Half-fill a cocktail shaker with ice. Add the schnapps, vodka, and lime juice. Shake vigorously and strain into a chilled martini glass. Garnish with a floating apple slice and spirals of lime.

The martini takes a Japanese twist with a bracing shot of sake.

saketini

Ice cubes
1/2 oz. sake
21/2 oz. vodka
Dash of dry vermouth
Thin cucumber baton

Half-fill a mixing glass with ice. Add the sake, vodka, and a dash of dry vermouth. Stir, then strain into a chilled martini glass and garnish with a thin baton of cucumber.

One sip and you'll be in the land of the lotus eaters.

lychee and peach martini

6 fresh lychees, peeled and seeded
1/2 oz. sugar syrup
Ice cubes
2 oz. peach-infused vodka (see recipe on page 25)
1 teaspoon lychee liqueur

Muddle five of the lychees with the sugar syrup in a cocktail shaker. Add a scoop of ice, then the vodka and lychee liqueur. Shake vigorously and strain into a chilled martini glass. Garnish with the remaining lychee on a wooden skewer.

sour apple martini

For a retro revival, garnish this sharp classic with sweet segments of canned mandarin.

mandarini martini

Ice cubes
2 oz. mandarin vodka
1/3 oz. dry vermouth
1/2 oz. cranberry juice
Orange twist

Half-fill a mixing glass with ice. Add the vodka, dry vermouth, and cranberry juice. Stir, strain into a chilled martini glass, and garnish with a twist of orange.

Associated in myth with lust and abduction, the purplish pomegranate is a seedy customer indeed.

pomegranate martini

3 tablespoons pomegranate seeds
1/2 oz. sugar syrup
Ice cubes
1 1/2 oz. bison grass vodka
1/2 oz. aperol
1/3 oz. apple juice
6 pomegranate seeds

Muddle the pomegranate seeds with the sugar syrup in a cocktail shaker. Add a scoop of ice, then the vodka, aperol, and apple juice. Shake vigorously and strain into a chilled martini glass. Garnish with pomegranate seeds.

Pale and herbal, dry vermouth is also called "French vermouth." This French kiss is not for the faint of heart.

gin and French

Ice cubes
2^1/$_3$ oz. gin
2/3 oz. dry vermouth
Lemon twist

Half-fill a mixing glass with ice. Add the gin and vermouth, then strain into a chilled cocktail glass. Garnish with a twist of lemon.

Say *buon giorno* to the Italian version of the gin and French.

It's sweet, red, and spicy and it'll knock your socks off.

gin and It

2 1/3 oz. gin
2/3 oz. sweet red vermouth
Maraschino cherry

Pour the gin and vermouth unchilled into a cocktail glass. Garnish with
a maraschino cherry.

mandarini martini

Once the drink of free-thinking, high-spirited girls about town,

it's high time to put the Gibson's name back up in lights.

Gibson

Ice cubes
2 3/4 oz. gin
1/3 oz. dry vermouth
Pearl onion

Half-fill a mixing glass with ice. Add the gin and vermouth, then stir. Strain
into a chilled cocktail glass and garnish with a pearl onion.

This celebrated cocktail takes its name from the New York hotel where the first martini was reputedly mixed.

Knickerbocker

Ice cubes
1/2 oz. dry vermouth
1/2 oz. sweet vermouth
2 oz. gin
Slice of lemon

Half-fill a mixing glass with ice. Add the dry vermouth, sweet vermouth, and gin. Strain into a chilled martini glass, squeeze a slice of lemon over the glass, and add the squeezed lemon to the cocktail.

Schoolgirl crushes are a thing of the past when the grown-up version tastes so much sweeter.

Campari crush

Crushed ice
1 oz. gin
1 oz. Campari
Ruby-red grapefruit juice
Lime wedge

Fill a highball glass with crushed ice. Add the gin and Campari, then top up with grapefruit juice. Squeeze a lime wedge into the glass and add the squeezed wedge to the drink.

You either love it or hate it, but the bitterly complex negroni has legion fans, having graced menus for close to a century.

negroni

Ice cubes
1 oz. gin
1 oz. sweet vermouth
1 oz. Campari
Club soda (optional)
Orange twist

Half-fill a mixing glass with ice. Add the gin, vermouth, and Campari. Stir well, then strain into a chilled cocktail glass. Add a dash of club soda if you wish. Garnish with a twist of orange.

Campari crush

Enough to make a maiden blush, this zesty cocktail is specially formulated to drown a lady's sorrows.

citrus blush

Crushed ice
1/2 oz. lime juice
1/2 oz. limoncello
1 1/2 oz. gin
Ruby-red grapefruit juice
Lime twist

Half-fill a tall glass with crushed ice. Add the lime juice, limoncello, and gin. Stir well to combine, top up with ruby-red grapefruit juice, and garnish with a twist of lime.

As stylized as its namesake, this drink puts on an impressive show. If you have too many, you will too.

kabuki

Lemon wedge
Salt
2 oz. sake
1/2 oz. lime juice cordial
1/2 oz. sugar syrup
1/2 oz. lime juice
1/2 oz. Cointreau
6 ice cubes
Lime twist

Wipe the lemon wedge around the rim of a martini glass, then dip the rim in salt to coat. Chill the glass. Place the sake, lime juice cordial, sugar syrup, lime juice, Cointreau, and ice in a heavy-duty blender. Blend well and pour into the prepared glass. Garnish with a twist of lime.

Sally forth on a united front and raise a toast to Italy's favorite general.

Garibaldi

1 1/2 oz. Campari
Ice cubes
Orange juice
Half an orange slice

Pour the Campari into a highball glass over ice, then top up with orange juice. Garnish with half a slice of orange.

When you're pouring drinks for a tough guy, knock him out with a taste of the Bronx.

Bronx

Ice cubes
1 oz. gin
1/2 oz. sweet red vermouth
1/2 oz. dry vermouth
1/2 oz. orange juice
Strawberry

Half-fill a cocktail shaker with ice. Add the gin, sweet red vermouth, dry vermouth, and orange juice. Shake well, then strain into a chilled cocktail glass. Garnish with a strawberry.

citrus blush

This cocktail is every bit as elegant and frosty as it sounds.

One to order when you're going for the ice-maiden look.

white lady

Ice cubes
1¹/2 oz. gin
1 oz. Cointreau
¹/2 oz. lemon juice
Dash of egg white (optional)

Half-fill a cocktail shaker with ice. Add the gin, Cointreau, lemon juice, and egg white. Shake well, then strain into a chilled cocktail glass.

What could be more sophisticated? A cosmopolitan should only be drunk when wearing a sassy smile and killer heels.

cosmopolitan

Ice cubes
1 1/2 oz. citrus vodka
1 oz. Cointreau
1/2 oz. cranberry juice
1/3 oz. lime juice
Lime twist

Half-fill a cocktail shaker with ice. Add the vodka, Cointreau, cranberry juice, and lime juice. Shake well and strain into a large, chilled martini glass. Garnish with a twist of lime.

Check the current, set your sails, and let the ocean winds take you where they will.

seabreeze

Ice cubes
1 1/2 oz. vodka
2 oz. cranberry juice
2 oz. ruby-red grapefruit juice
1/2 oz. lime juice
Lime twist

Half-fill a cocktail shaker with ice. Add the vodka, cranberry juice, grapefruit juice, and lime juice. Shake well and strain into a highball glass half-filled with ice. Garnish with a twist of lime.

Amble through this cocktail as you would a rambling orchard on a clear, sunny day.

life's good

Ice cubes
1 1/2 oz. sloe berry vodka
1/2 oz. lychee juice
1/2 oz. cranberry juice
1/2 oz. strawberry purée (see recipe on page 23)
Lime wedge

Half-fill a cocktail shaker with ice. Add the vodka, lychee juice, cranberry juice, and strawberry purée. Shake vigorously and strain into a chilled martini glass. Squeeze the lime wedge over the drink and add it as a garnish.

BARTENDER'S TIP For an after-dinner drink, sprinkle with grated chocolate.

life's good

Seems docile enough, but beware the mighty kick.

Moscow mule

Ice cubes
1 1/2 oz. vodka
1/2 oz. lime juice
Nonalcoholic ginger beer
Lime wedge

Half-fill a highball glass with ice. Add the vodka and lime juice, then top
up with ginger beer and garnish with a wedge of lime.

Warning: this mule *bites* as well as kicks!

ginger and cranberry mule

Crushed ice
2 oz. vodka
1/2 cup frozen cranberries
2 1/2 oz. nonalcoholic ginger beer
3/4 cup cranberry juice

Fill two highball glasses three-quarters full with crushed ice. Divide the vodka and cranberries between the glasses. In a mixing glass, mix together the ginger beer and cranberry juice and pour over the vodka. Serves 2.

Bison grass has reputed aphrodisiac qualities—for buffaloes at least. Who knows what a shot or two might do for you?

bison kick

Ice cubes
1 1/2 oz. bison grass vodka
1/3 oz. sake
1 oz. watermelon juice
1/2 oz. lychee juice
1/3 oz. sugar syrup
1 peeled fresh lychee

Half-fill a cocktail shaker with ice. Add the vodka, sake, watermelon juice, lychee juice, and sugar syrup. Shake vigorously and strain into a chilled cocktail glass. Garnish with a lychee.

Crank up your courage, release the throttle, and go down in a blaze of glory.

kamikaze

Ice cubes
1 1/2 oz. vodka
1/2 oz. Cointreau
1 oz. lemon juice
Dash of lime juice cordial

Half-fill a cocktail shaker with ice. Add the vodka, Cointreau, lemon juice, and lime juice cordial. Shake well and strain into a chilled cocktail glass. Garnish with a cocktail umbrella.

bison kick

Too many Suzy Wongs and you'll be up at the mic singing woozy songs.

Suzy Wong

Ice cubes
1 1/2 oz. citrus vodka
1 teaspoon lime juice
1 teaspoon sugar syrup
1 1/2 oz. watermelon juice
Lime twist

Fill a mixing glass with ice. Add the vodka, lime juice, sugar syrup, and watermelon juice. Stir, then strain into a chilled cocktail glass. Garnish with a twist of lime.

After you're done mangling woozy songs, take a short break and muddle your way through a mint wong.

mint wong

5 small chunks of watermelon
8 mint leaves
1/2 oz. sugar syrup
Ice cubes
1 1/2 oz. citrus vodka
1/2 oz. cranberry juice

Muddle the watermelon and mint with the sugar syrup in a cocktail shaker. Add a scoop of ice, then the vodka and cranberry juice. Shake vigorously and pour into a chilled tumbler.

Woo! Woo! Chattanooga, here we come! A few of these down your gullet and you'll be flying along.

WOO WOO

Ice cubes
Lime wedge
2 oz. vodka
1/2 oz. peach schnapps
Cranberry juice

Half-fill a cocktail shaker with ice. Squeeze the lime wedge into the shaker, then add the vodka and peach schnapps. Shake, then strain into an old-fashioned glass half-filled with ice. Add the squeezed lime wedge and top up with cranberry juice.

The blueberry of happiness brightens up old Tom's
club lounge classic.

berry collins

3 tablespoons blueberries
1/2 oz. sugar syrup
Ice cubes
1 1/2 oz. gin
1 oz. vanilla liqueur
1/2 oz. lemon juice
Cranberry juice or lemonade

Muddle the blueberries with the sugar syrup in a cocktail shaker. Add a
scoop of ice, then the gin, vanilla liqueur, and lemon juice. Shake
vigorously and pour into a tall glass to 1 inch from the top, then top up
with cranberry juice or lemonade.

berry collins

jungle juice Forget the concrete jungle, we're off to the rum jungle on a high-spirited cocktail safari, so grab your pith helmet and insect repellent and get ready for some wild nights—no passing out allowed.

Just remember that jungle potions have potent effects—imbibe too many and you might start seeing pink elephants. Now turn the music up a notch, it's time to jungle boogie! Get down, get down . . .

This is a story about rambunctious rum runners, punch-happy persuaders, cool customers from the Caribbean, and their Mexican friends—a gang of heavy-duty party troopers who know how to get things started! Their fiery, fruity prescriptions will rev up the action at the drop of a hat and inspire bouts of revelry and even devilry. Essential supplies for this bacchanalian adventure include rum aplenty, both dark and white, from standard to overproof intensity. Procure several bottles of tequila for slamming down some wicked margaritas, and a generous supply of gin and vodka. A few heady punches call for ingredients such as bubbly red wine, Pimm's No. 1, bourbon, and sweet vermouth. It's bound to get hot, so keep buckets of ice on hand, as well as thirst quenchers such as tonic water (to fend off malaria), club soda, cola, lemonade, and ginger ale. Deep in the jungle, pluck a fresh harvest of limes, lemons, pineapples, and oranges to squeeze into your drinks. Other reviving essences include Angostura bitters, sugar syrup, fruit brandies, and fruity liqueurs (black currant, banana, strawberry, melon), amaretto, Cointreau, Grand Marnier, Galliano, and the dark, mysterious Kahlúa. Blue curaçao, green Chartreuse, green crème de menthe, and grenadine are the secret to the exquisite bird-of-paradise colors glimpsed in our potions, the likes of which are rarely seen. So let our journey begin.

Beg, borrow, or steal a traditional crystal punch bowl to serve this heady punch.

planter's punch

Ice cubes
2 cups dark rum
3/4 cup lime juice
3/4 cup lemon juice
1/4 cup superfine sugar
1 teaspoon Angostura bitters
2 cups club soda
Fresh fruit slices, such as kiwifruit and pineapple

One-third fill a large punch bowl with ice. Pour in the rum, lime juice, lemon juice, sugar, and bitters. Mix well, then top up with club soda and garnish with slices of fresh fruit. Serves 10.

BARTENDER'S TIP Some people like to add mint leaves and cucumber slices to their punch.

Music and passion will soon be the fashion when you send out a round of these!

Copacabana punch

2³/4 oz. gin
2³/4 oz. white rum
2 cups champagne or sparkling wine
4 cups pineapple juice
1 cup finely diced pineapple
1/2 cup passion fruit pulp
20 mint leaves

Pour the gin, rum, champagne or sparkling wine, and pineapple juice into a large pitcher or punch bowl. Add the diced pineapple, passion fruit pulp, and mint leaves. Add enough ice cubes to fill the pitcher, stir gently to combine, and serve in chilled glasses. Serves 10.

Family celebrations call for a certain caliber of drink. Here's a wickedly simple way to keep the peace.

Pimm's punch

1¹/₂ cups orange juice
Ice cubes
1²/₃ cups Pimm's No. 1
1²/₃ cups bourbon
³/₄ cup sweet vermouth

³/₄ cup white rum
1 bottle of champagne or
    sparkling wine
3 cups chopped fresh fruit

Freeze ¹/₃ cup of the orange juice in an ice-cube tray. Half-fill a punch bowl with ice, then add the Pimm's, bourbon, vermouth, rum, remaining orange juice, and the champagne or sparkling wine. Stir in the fresh fruit and the frozen orange-juice ice cubes. Serves 10.

While away a lazy afternoon with a good pal and a pitcher
of fruity sangria.

sangria

1/2 oz. lemon juice	11/2 oz. gin
1/2 oz. orange juice	11/2 oz. vodka
2 tablespoons superfine	1 lemon
sugar	1 orange
1 bottle of red wine	1 lime
21/2 cups lemonade	Ice cubes

Put the lemon juice, orange juice, and sugar in a large pitcher or bowl and
stir until the sugar has dissolved. Add the red wine, lemonade, gin, and
vodka. Cut a lemon, an orange, and a lime in half, remove the seeds,
and slice finely. Add the fruit to the pitcher, fill with ice, stir, and serve.
Serves 10.

Pimm's punch

In Tahitian, *mai tai* roughly translates as "out of this world."
After just one mai tai, you too will be out of this world.

mai tai

Crushed ice	3 oz. pineapple juice
1 oz. white rum	3 oz. orange juice
1 oz. dark rum	1/2 oz. sugar syrup
1/2 oz. Cointreau	Dash of grenadine
1/2 oz. amaretto	Lime slice
1/2 oz. lemon juice	Mint leaves

Half-fill a large goblet glass with crushed ice. Add the white rum, dark rum, Cointreau, amaretto, lemon juice, pineapple juice, orange juice, sugar syrup, and grenadine. Stir, then garnish with a slice of lime and some fresh mint leaves.

This utterly stupefying drink should be ingested with caution—unless you wish to join the ranks of the walking dead!

zombie

Ice cubes
1 oz. white rum
1 oz. dark rum
1 oz. overproof rum
1/2 oz. apricot brandy
1/2 oz. cherry brandy

2 oz. orange juice
1/2 oz. lime juice
Fresh fruit

Half-fill a cocktail shaker with ice. Add all the rum, the apricot brandy, cherry brandy, orange juice, and lime juice. Shake well and strain into a highball glass over ice. Garnish with fresh fruit and serve with a straw.

Exquisitely refreshing, this Caribbean classic is excellent for the constitution, as well as the conversation.

Bacardi cocktail

Ice cubes
2 oz. white Bacardi rum
1 oz. lemon or lime juice
1/3 oz. grenadine
Maraschino cherry

Half-fill a cocktail shaker with ice. Add the Bacardi, lemon or lime juice, and grenadine, then shake well and strain into a chilled cocktail glass. Garnish with a maraschino cherry.

Throw off the shackles, free your mind, and embrace the spirit of revolution.

Cuba libre

Ice cubes
2 oz. white rum
6 lime wedges
Cola
Lime wedge

Half-fill a highball glass with ice. Add the rum, squeeze the lime wedges into the glass, and then add the squeezed wedges to the drink. Top up with cola and garnish with a wedge of lime.

Cuba libre

Party people the world over know how to shake the place up.
They're the ones wielding a shaken margarita.

margarita (shaken)

2 lime wedges
Salt
Ice cubes
1 1/2 oz. tequila
1/2 oz. Cointreau
1/2 oz. lemon juice
1/2 oz. lime juice
Dash of sugar syrup

Run a wedge of lime around the rim of a cocktail glass. Dip the rim into a saucer of salt, shaking off any excess. Chill the glass. Half-fill a cocktail shaker with ice and add the tequila, Cointreau, lemon juice, lime juice, and sugar syrup. Shake well, then strain into the salt-frosted cocktail glass. Garnish with the remaining wedge of lime.

For your next party trick, serve these up in shot glasses with the salt and lemon on the side.

margarita (frozen)

2 lime wedges
Salt
1 cup crushed ice
1 1/2 oz. tequila
1/2 oz. Cointreau
1/2 oz. lemon juice
1/2 oz. lime juice
Dash of sugar syrup

Run a wedge of lime around the rim of a cocktail glass. Dip the rim in a saucer of salt, shaking off any excess. Chill the glass. Place the crushed ice, tequila, Cointreau, lemon juice, lime juice, and sugar syrup in a blender. Blend until the mixture is the consistency of shaved ice, pour into the salt-frosted cocktail glass, and garnish with the remaining wedge of lime.

Recapture the glow of the golden days with this perenially popular party elixir.

golden margarita

Lime wedge
Salt
1 cup crushed ice
1 1/2 oz. tequila
1/2 oz. Grand Marnier
1/2 oz. orange juice
1/2 oz. lime juice
Orange twist

Run a wedge of lime around the rim of a cocktail glass. Dip the rim in a saucer of salt, shaking off any excess. Chill the glass. Place the crushed ice, tequila, Grand Marnier, orange juice, and lime juice in a blender and blend until the mixture is the consistency of shaved ice. Pour into the salt-frosted cocktail glass and garnish with an orange twist.

There's a little devil in all of us just yearning to be set free with a glass of sparkling potion.

el diablo

Ice cubes
2 oz. tequila
1 oz. black currant liqueur
Ginger ale
Lime wedge

Half-fill an old-fashioned glass with ice, add the tequila and black currant liqueur, then top up with ginger ale. Squeeze the lime wedge into the glass and add the squeezed wedge to the drink. Stir.

el diablo

Sprinkle the salt where you want to be licked and start a round of party games.

tequila slammer

1 oz. tequila
Ginger ale or lemonade

Pour the tequila into a shot glass and top up with ginger ale or lemonade.

Sunrise is a scary sight when you still have a margarita in your hand.

tequila sunrise

Ice cubes
1 oz. tequila
Orange juice
Dash of grenadine
Orange twist

Half-fill a highball glass with ice. Add the tequila and top up with orange juice. Add the grenadine by carefully pouring it over the back of a spoon. Garnish with a twist of orange.

It's a brave babe who waves the red flag, but several of these should steel your nerve.

brave bull

Ice cubes
1 oz. Kahlúa
1 1/2 oz. tequila

Half-fill an old-fashioned glass with ice. Add the Kahlúa, then the tequila. Swirl gently before drinking.

South of the border, the party starts early and finishes late.
Celebrate with a local shout.

olé

Ice cubes
1 1/2 oz. tequila
1 oz. banana liqueur
Dash of blue curaçao

Half-fill a cocktail shaker with ice. Add the tequila and banana liqueur, then shake well. Strain into a small, chilled cocktail glass. Tip a dash of blue curaçao into the drink to achieve a two-tone effect.

olé

Whatever you do, don't try to order another one of these after you've finished the first.

Freddie Fudpucker

Ice cubes
1 1/2 oz. tequila
1/2 oz. Galliano
2 oz. orange juice
Half an orange slice
Maraschino cherry

Half-fill a cocktail shaker with ice. Add the tequila, Galliano, and orange juice, shake vigorously, and strain into a chilled cocktail glass. Garnish with half a slice of orange and a maraschino cherry.

Whatever issues Harvey may have had with that wall, it certainly resulted in a classic drink.

Harvey Wallbanger

Crushed ice
1 oz. vodka
⅓ oz. Galliano
Orange juice
Half an orange slice

Half-fill a highball glass with crushed ice. Add the vodka and Galliano, then top up with orange juice. Garnish with half a slice of orange.

Fast cars and fast women make for a racy evening. For a *flaming* good time, momentarily light the Chartreuse before drinking.

Lamborghini

1/2 oz. Kahlúa
1/2 oz. Galliano
1/2 oz. green Chartreuse

Pour the Kahlúa into a port or sherry glass, then carefully float the Galliano on top by pouring it over the back of a teaspoon. Using a clean teaspoon, float the green Chartreuse over the Galliano to create three distinct layers.

If your day barely made it out of first gear, line up a rack of these and go, go, go.

traffic lights

1/2 oz. banana liqueur
1/2 oz. strawberry liqueur
1/2 oz. melon liqueur

Pour the banana liqueur into a shot glass, then carefully float the strawberry liqueur on top by pouring it over the back of a teaspoon. Using a clean teaspoon, float the melon liqueur over the strawberry liqueur to create three distinct layers.

Harvey Wallbanger

Stash this powerful medicine in your first-aid kit and reserve for an emergency kick-start.

corpse reviver

Ice cubes
1 oz. brandy
1 oz. Calvados
1 oz. sweet vermouth
Apple slices

Half-fill a cocktail shaker with ice. Add the brandy, Calvados, and vermouth, shake vigorously, and strain into a chilled cocktail glass. Garnish with apple slices.

Possibly not the only reptile you'll meet at the bar,

but certainly the greenest.

screaming lizard

Ice cubes
1 oz. green crème de menthe
1 oz. green Chartreuse
1 oz. club soda

Place some ice in a tumbler. Add the crème de menthe, Chartreuse, and
club soda, then stir.

An experience to be shared only with someone you really, really, really like.

.

between the sheets

Ice cubes
1 oz. white rum
1 oz. brandy
1 oz. Cointreau
Dash of lemon juice
Lemon twist

Half-fill a cocktail shaker with ice. Add the rum, brandy, Cointreau, and lemon juice and shake well. Strain into a chilled cocktail glass and garnish with a twist of lemon.

Raid the high-school science lab for an authentic wooden test-tube rack to serve up these sweet little darlings.

test-tube baby

1/2 oz. amaretto
1/2 oz. tequila
2 drops Irish cream

Pour the amaretto into a shot glass or a clean test tube, then carefully float the tequila on top by pouring it over the back of a teaspoon. Add the Irish cream.

corpse reviver

froufrou Frills and thrills galore for those who want a little afternoon delight or a fleeting flirtation with sweetness and light. From the decadently opulent to the wildly whimsical, nothing here is to be

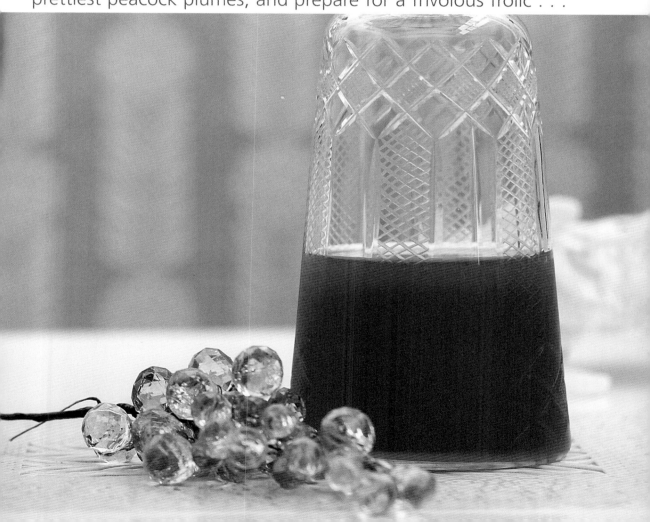

taken too seriously. It's high time to flaunt it, so get ready for a full-on fanfare! Flounce about in your flashiest feathers, primp and preen your prettiest peacock plumes, and prepare for a frivolous frolic . . .

This chapter could almost be described as a midsummer night's dream. So let us introduce a tutti-frutti cast of players whose sole mission is to entice the senses and tickle the most fantastical of fancies—to utterly delight, indulge, and entertain. What follows is a kaleidoscope of technicolor dreams, featuring a vast, eclectic troop of royal luminaries such as champagne, Cointreau, Pernod, and Parfait Amour, cameo appearances by instantly recognizable types such as gin, vodka, and white rum (clearly lowlifes!), a gamut of resplendent liqueurs (melon, peach, strawberry, banana, and chocolate)—an ensemble superbly supported by notables such as amaretto, cherry brandy, Sambuca, Malibu, green crème de menthe, white crème de cacao, and blue curaçao. Keeping up appearances is integral to the show, with many a flamboyant flourish anticipated from exotic fruits and maraschino cherries; expect juicy performances and an acerbic wit from limes, lemons, and pineapples. Plot thickeners include agents as diverse as sugar syrup, rose water, grenadine, Angostura bitters, raspberry cordial, lemonade, and apple cider. And for comic relief, don't miss a rib-tickling appearance by a licorice allsort and a jelly bean! All in all, a glittering show at once zany, capricious, and wanton, guaranteed to make you feel for one tizzy, giddy moment gloriously and unashamedly chichi. So let the show begin . . .

Greet the glitterati with these jewel-studded Jell-O shots and watch their jaws drop.

champagne and lychee Jell-O shots

1/2 oz. sugar syrup
1/2 cup champagne or sparkling wine
3/4 teaspoon powdered gelatin
3 lychees, peeled, seeded, and halved
6 raspberries

Heat the sugar syrup and champagne or sparkling wine until just hot. Mix 1 tablespoon of the hot liquid with the gelatin until smooth, then stir into the remaining liquid until the gelatin is dissolved. Cool, then place half a lychee and a raspberry into six shot glasses. Pour in the champagne mixture and chill for 3 hours or until set. Makes 6.

Parfait Amour speaks in hushed tones of simmering, ardent passions. In a frappé it is a pure frisson of love.

frappé

Crushed ice
1/2 oz. Parfait Amour
1/2 oz. Cointreau

Fill a large goblet with crushed ice, then pour over the Parfait Amour and Cointreau. Serve with a short straw or a long-handled spoon.

Make like the bright young things of the Roaring Twenties and dazzle the boys with this snappy number.

strawberry flapper

4 hulled strawberries
4 ice cubes
1/2 oz. strawberry liqueur
Chilled champagne or sparkling wine

Place the strawberries, ice cubes, and strawberry liqueur in a heavy-duty blender, then blend until smooth. Pour into a chilled champagne flute and slowly top up with champagne or sparkling wine.

This magical version of a childhood classic could have slipped straight out of the pages of *Alice in Wonderland*.

raspberry champagne spider

1–2 raspberry sorbet balls
Chilled champagne or sparkling wine

Place one or two balls of raspberry sorbet in a chilled champagne flute and slowly top up with champagne or sparkling wine.

BARTENDER'S TIP Scoop a tub of raspberry sorbet into small balls with a melon baller and freeze until needed.

raspberry champagne spider

When the occasion calls for utter decadence—and even when it doesn't.

watermelon and rose water martini

5 chunks of watermelon
1/2 oz. sugar syrup
Ice cubes
2 oz. watermelon-infused vodka (see recipe on page 25)
3 drops of rose water
3 rose petals

Muddle the watermelon with the sugar syrup in a cocktail shaker. Add a scoop of ice, then the vodka and rose water. Shake vigorously and strain into a chilled martini glass. Garnish with floating rose petals.

These martinis are so great, you could drink a whole bunch of them.

grape martini

6 red grapes
6 white grapes
1/2 oz. sugar syrup
Ice cubes
2 oz. vodka

Muddle five red and five white grapes with the sugar syrup in a cocktail shaker. Add a scoop of ice and the vodka. Shake vigorously and strain into a chilled martini glass. Garnish with the remaining red and white grapes on a wooden skewer.

This glorious explosion of color and flavor will knock you all the way to kingdom come.

cherry bombe

Ice cubes	Dash of grenadine
1/2 oz. gin	Dash of Angostura bitters
1/2 oz. cherry brandy	Pineapple juice
1/2 oz. lime juice	Pineapple wedge
1/2 oz. Cointreau	Pineapple leaves

Half-fill a cocktail shaker with ice. Add the gin, cherry brandy, lime juice, Cointreau, a dash of grenadine, and a dash of bitters. Shake well and strain into a highball glass half-filled with ice. Top up with pineapple juice and garnish with a pineapple wedge and pineapple leaves.

When you start seeing little green men, use your melon and offer them this intergalactic fantasy.

cider with Midori and floating melon bombes

1 small honeydew melon
3/4 cup Midori
3 cups chilled alcoholic apple cider

Scoop the honeydew melon into small balls with a melon baller and freeze for several hours until solid. Divide the Midori among four small to medium tumblers, then carefully pour in the cider to half-fill the glasses. Top with the frozen melon balls. Serves 4.

watermelon and rose water martini

No one will ever blow raspberries at this bloomin' beautiful extravaganza.

red blossom

Ice cubes
1 1/2 oz. gin
1/2 oz. peach liqueur
3 tablespoons raspberries
1/2 oz. lemon juice
1/2 oz. sugar syrup
3 blueberries

Add a scoop of ice to a cocktail shaker, then the gin, peach liqueur, raspberries, lemon juice, and sugar syrup. Shake vigorously and strain into a chilled martini glass. Garnish with blueberries.

Love, sweet love, can so easily turn sour, but this old faithful will never let you down.

per f'amour

Ice cubes
1/2 oz. Cointreau
1/2 oz. Parfait Amour
1 1/2 oz. orange juice
Dash of egg white
Orange twist

Half-fill a cocktail shaker with ice. Add the Cointreau, Parfait Amour, orange juice, and a dash of egg white. Shake well until frothy, then strain into a chilled martini glass. Garnish with a twist of orange.

Candy sweet and cute as a button—just remember this one is *not* for the kiddies!

jelly bean

Ice cubes
1/2 oz. Sambuca
1/3 oz. raspberry cordial
Lemonade
Jelly beans

Fill a cocktail glass with ice. Add the Sambuca and raspberry cordial, then top up with lemonade. Garnish with jelly beans.

It takes allsorts to make the world go round, but not too many to set it spinning!

licorice allsort

Ice cubes
1/2 oz. black Sambuca
1/2 oz. strawberry liqueur
1/2 oz. Malibu
2 oz. cream
Licorice allsort or multicolored confectionery

Half-fill a cocktail shaker with ice. Add the black Sambuca, strawberry liqueur, Malibu, and cream and shake well. Strain into a chilled cocktail glass and garnish with a licorice allsort or other confectionery on the rim.

red blossom

Many a maiden has lost her modesty because of this seemingly innocent drink.

lost cherry

1/2 oz. Malibu
1/2 oz. strawberry liqueur
1/2 oz. chocolate liqueur
1 oz. cream
Half a chocolate-coated cherry bar
1 cup crushed ice
Chocolate-dipped stemmed cocktail cherries or fresh cherries

Pour the Malibu, strawberry liqueur, chocolate liqueur, and cream into a blender, then add the chocolate-coated cherry bar and blend until smooth. Add the crushed ice and blend until the drink is the consistency of shaved ice. Pour into a large, chilled cocktail glass and garnish with cherries on skewers.

Your halo may have slipped a little, but this heavenly creation will give you wings.

fallen angel

Ice cubes
1 1/2 oz. gin
1/2 oz. green crème de menthe
1 oz. lemon juice
Dash of Angostura bitters
Maraschino cherry

Half-fill a cocktail shaker with ice. Add the gin, crème de menthe, lemon juice, and bitters, then shake vigorously. Strain into a chilled cocktail glass and garnish with a maraschino cherry.

East meets West in this sophisticated fusion of egg and nog.

Japanese eggnog

Ice cubes
1¹/₂ oz. Cointreau
1¹/₂ oz. melon liqueur
2³/₄ oz. milk
Dash of egg white

Half-fill a cocktail shaker with ice. Add the Cointreau, melon liqueur, milk, and egg white, then shake well. Strain into a chilled cocktail glass.

Reorient yourself and sip into something really comforting.

Japanese slipper

Ice cubes
1 oz. melon liqueur
1 oz. Cointreau
1/2 oz. lemon juice
Maraschino cherry

Half-fill a cocktail shaker with ice. Add the melon liqueur, Cointreau, and lemon juice. Shake well and strain into a chilled cocktail glass. Garnish with a maraschino cherry.

Japanese slipper

Better throw this one down quickly before it disappears.

Whoops, it just did!

mirage

Ice cubes
1/2 oz. lime juice
1/2 oz. melon liqueur
31/2 oz. nonalcoholic ginger beer
1/2 oz. vodka
1/2 oz. strawberry liqueur
Lime slice

Fill a highball glass with ice one-third full. Add the lime juice, melon liqueur, and ginger beer. Mix the vodka and strawberry liqueur in a separate glass, then gently float the vodka mixture onto the ginger beer by pouring it over the back of a teaspoon. Garnish with a slice of lime.

Definitely not a milkshake for the kiddies, this concoction has a touch of the exotic.

Japanese shake

Ice cubes
1/2 oz. melon liqueur
1/2 oz. banana liqueur
1/2 oz. white crème de cacao
2 oz. cream
stemmed cocktail cherry

Half-fill a cocktail shaker with ice. Add the melon liqueur, banana liqueur, crème de cacao, and cream. Shake well, then strain into a chilled cocktail glass. Garnish with a cocktail cherry.

Recommended for internal use only, this frothy formulation is guaranteed to leave no tears.

shampoo

½ oz. gin
½ oz. lemon juice
Dash of Pernod
Dash of blue curaçao
Chilled champagne or sparkling wine
Lemon twist

Pour the gin, then the lemon juice, Pernod, and blue curaçao into a chilled champagne flute. Slowly top up with champagne or sparkling wine and garnish with a twist of lemon.

When the green-eyed monster strikes, give the savage beast a dose of its own medicine.

envy

Ice cubes
1/2 oz. white rum
1/2 oz. amaretto
1/2 oz. blue curaçao
1/2 oz. lime juice
2 3/4 oz. pineapple juice
Pineapple wedge

Half-fill a cocktail shaker with ice. Add the rum, amaretto, blue curaçao, lime juice, and pineapple juice. Shake well, then strain into a highball glass half-filled with ice. Garnish with a wedge of pineapple.

shampoo

tropicana Imagine yourself in an equatorial loveland sequestered from worries, sipping like a giant hummingbird on precious nectars extracted from the rampant fruits of the warm wet earth. Wear a flower in your hair and feel the sensual island breeze caress your cheeks. Marvel at the mighty sun's slow trajectory through the sky and at its fiery demise. This is the island time forgot. Welcome to paradise.

When the antics of this maddening world start to drive you bananas and make you lose your coconuts, you know you need to pack up your bongos and go tropical for a while. Extract yourself from the feverish melee and tune in to island time, where life has a slower, stronger pulse and moves at a leisurely pace. Feel the slow crash of the surf on the beach, dig your toes deep into fine, white, squeaky-clean sand, and then administer some strong tropical medicines such as rum and tequila in the form of a daiquiri, margarita, or piña colada. For the full island experience, don't forget the Grand Marnier, Cointreau, Galliano, Malibu, Kahlúa, and crème de cacao, and don't skimp on the cream, milk, and coconut cream. The pounding sun and soaring mercury can challenge the equanimity, but mercifully this is an abundant place, where fruits and berries grow in jungly profusion to slake your thirst and keep you cool. Celebrate nature's bounty with fruity liqueurs and purées in a rainbow of flavors. Even our "dear little water" vodka is infused with luscious essences—citrus, peach, vanilla, and currants. Other essential requirements in this magical place are a cargo hold of cold, cold ice, cocktail umbrellas, a deck chair, sarong (or a grass skirt if you prefer), an outlandish pair of sunglasses, a flouncy broad-rimmed hat, and a nice pair of lovely hands to rub some sunscreen into those out-of-the-way spots. Aloha, heaven.

A tempting taste of paradise in every tiny shot.

passion fruit and vanilla vodka Jell-O shots

1/2 oz. sugar syrup
2¾ oz. passion fruit pulp
¾ teaspoon powdered gelatin
2¾ oz. vanilla vodka

Heat the sugar syrup and passion fruit pulp until just hot. Mix 1 tablespoon of the hot liquid with the gelatin until smooth, then stir into the remaining liquid until the gelatin is dissolved.Cool, stir in the vodka, and pour into six shot glasses. Refrigerate for 3 hours or until set. Makes 6.

Make these in the prettiest shot glasses you can find!

orange Jell-O shots

1/2 oz. sugar syrup
23/4 oz. pulp-free orange juice
1/2 oz. lemon juice
3/4 teaspoon powdered gelatin
2 oz. Grand Marnier
1/2 oz. Galliano
6 orange segments

Heat the sugar syrup, orange juice, and lemon juice until just hot. Mix 1 tablespoon of the hot liquid with the gelatin until smooth, then stir into the remaining liquid until the gelatin is dissolved. Cool, then add the Grand Marnier and Galliano. Place an orange segment in six shot glasses and pour in the juice mixture. Refrigerate for 3 hours or until set. Makes 6.

A memorable way to melt the ice—better make it in bulk.

daiquiri (frozen)

1 cup crushed ice
1 1/2 oz. white rum
1 oz. lime juice
1/2 oz. sugar syrup
Lime twist

Place the crushed ice, rum, lime juice, and sugar syrup in a blender and blend until the mixture is the consistency of shaved ice. Pour into a chilled cocktail glass and garnish with a twist of lime.

Take it shaken and you may find yourself well stirred.

daiquiri (shaken)

Ice cubes
1 1/2 oz. white rum
1 oz. lime juice
1/2 oz. sugar syrup

Half-fill a cocktail shaker with ice. Add the rum, lime juice, and sugar syrup. Shake vigorously and strain into a chilled cocktail glass.

passion fruit and vanilla vodka Jell-O shots

Listen to the calypso rhythms in your mind, jump into the nearest banana boat, and find your island in the sun.

banana daiquiri

Half a banana, peeled
1 oz. white rum
1/2 oz. banana liqueur
1/2 oz. lime juice
1/2 oz. sugar syrup
1 cup crushed ice
Banana slice, dipped in lemon juice

Place the banana, rum, banana liqueur, lime juice, and sugar syrup in a blender and blend until smooth. Add the crushed ice and blend until the mixture is the consistency of shaved ice. Pour into a chilled cocktail glass and garnish with a slice of banana.

So very, very drinkable that you really should make a pitcher—
one will never be enough.

mango daiquiri

Half a mango, peeled and diced
1 oz. white rum
1/2 oz. mango liqueur
1/2 oz. lemon juice
1/2 oz. sugar syrup
1 cup crushed ice

Place the mango, rum, mango liqueur, lemon juice, and sugar syrup in a
blender and blend until smooth. Add the crushed ice and blend until the
mixture is the consistency of shaved ice. Pour into a chilled cocktail glass.

The fragrant sweetness of lychees lifts the humble daiquiri into the realms of legend.

pineapple, lychee, and mint daiquiri

4 mint leaves
1 1/2 oz. white rum
1/2 cup diced fresh pineapple
4 lychees, peeled and seeded
1/2 oz. pineapple juice

1/2 oz. lime juice
1/2 oz. sugar syrup
1 cup crushed ice
Pineapple leaves
Mint sprig

Place the mint, rum, pineapple, lychees, pineapple juice, lime juice, and sugar syrup in a blender. Add the crushed ice and blend until the mixture is the consistency of shaved ice. Pour into a large chilled cocktail glass and garnish with pineapple leaves and a sprig of mint.

Sipping this fruits-of-the-forest delight is like taking a ramble through the brambles with not a thorn in sight.

berry daiquiri

1/2 oz. white rum	4 fresh or frozen raspberries
1/2 oz. Cointreau	4 fresh or frozen blackberries
1/2 oz. raspberry liqueur	1 cup crushed ice
3 strawberries	Fresh or frozen berries

Place the rum, Cointreau, raspberry liqueur, strawberries, raspberries, and blackberries in a blender and blend until smooth. Add the crushed ice and blend until the mixture is the consistency of shaved ice. Pour the mixture into a chilled cocktail glass and garnish with fresh or frozen berries on a skewer.

pineapple, lychee, and mint daiquiri

Any time you want to impress the pants off somebody, wow them with this awesomely mesmerizing margarita.

blood-orange margarita

Egg white
Superfine sugar
Ice cubes
1 1/2 oz. gold tequila
1/2 oz. mandarin liqueur or
Grand Marnier

1/2 oz. lime juice
1 oz. blood-orange juice
1/3 oz. sugar syrup

Dip the rim of a cocktail glass in a saucer of egg white, then a saucer of sugar, shaking off any excess. Chill. Add a scoop of ice to a cocktail shaker, then the tequila, mandarin liqueur or Grand Marnier, lime juice, blood-orange juice, and sugar syrup. Shake vigorously and strain into the sugar-frosted cocktail glass.

Pretty in pink with a lemon-lime surprise, this sublime cocktail will smooth over any rough patch.

strawberry margarita

Lemon wedge
Salt
Crushed ice
1 oz. tequila
1/2 oz. strawberry liqueur

1/2 oz. Cointreau
1/2 oz. sugar syrup
1/2 oz. lemon juice
Strawberry half
Lemon slice

Run a lemon wedge around the rim of a cocktail glass. Dip the rim into a saucer of salt and chill. Blend the crushed ice, tequila, strawberry liqueur, Cointreau, sugar syrup, and lemon juice in a blender and pour into the salt-frosted cocktail glass. Garnish with a strawberry half and a slice of lemon.

Take a flight of fancy to the land of the long, white cloud.

kiwifruit margarita

Egg white
Superfine sugar
Crushed ice
1 1/2 oz. tequila
1/2 oz. Cointreau
1/2 oz. melon liqueur
1/2 oz. lemon juice
1–2 kiwifruits, peeled and chopped
Kiwifruit slice

Dip the rim of a cocktail glass in a saucer of egg white, then a saucer of sugar, shaking off any excess. Chill. Place the crushed ice, tequila, Cointreau, melon liqueur, lemon juice, and kiwifruit in a blender and blend well. Pour into the sugar-frosted cocktail glass and garnish with a slice of kiwifruit.

Resuscitate a flagging romance with a passionate fling.

passion fruit margarita

Egg white
Superfine sugar
Ice cubes
1¹/₂ oz. gold tequila
¹/₃ oz. Cointreau
1 oz. passion fruit purée
¹/₂ oz. lemon juice
¹/₂ oz. lime juice
¹/₃ oz. sugar syrup

Dip the rim of a cocktail glass in a saucer of egg white, then a saucer of sugar, shaking off any excess. Chill. Add a scoop of ice to a cocktail shaker, then the tequila, Cointreau, passion fruit purée, lemon juice, lime juice, and sugar syrup. Shake vigorously and strain into the sugar-rimmed cocktail glass.

kiwifruit margarita

After years of diligent service, the old martini meanders off into equatorial climes.

pineapple and ginger martini

6 chunks of pineapple
1/2 oz. sugar syrup
Ice cubes
2 oz. vodka
1/2 oz. ginger liqueur
Pineapple leaf

Muddle the pineapple with the sugar syrup in a cocktail shaker. Add a scoop of ice, then the vodka and ginger liqueur. Shake vigorously and strain into a chilled martini glass. Garnish with a pineapple leaf.

When the temperature starts getting hellishly hot, here's a diabolically delicious diversion for blasted palates.

diablo

Ice cubes
1¹/₂ oz. black currant vodka
1 oz. blackberry liqueur
1 oz. pineapple juice
Pineapple leaf

Add a scoop of ice to a cocktail shaker, then the vodka, blackberry liqueur, and pineapple juice. Shake vigorously and strain into a chilled martini glass. Garnish with a pineapple leaf.

Sip it on your favorite beach as the sun slips over the horizon or in your favorite chair as you sink into the evening.

Cointreau sunsets

Crushed ice
1/2 cup Cointreau
Dash of grenadine
1 2/3 cups orange juice
Dash of Angostura bitters

Fill four tall glasses with crushed ice. Divide the Cointreau among the glasses, add a dash of grenadine, and carefully top up with orange juice. Add a dash of bitters, to taste. Serves 4.

When the master of illusion strikes, clear your vision with a charge of this.

illusion

Ice cubes
1/2 oz. melon liqueur
1/2 oz. Cointreau
1/2 oz. vodka
1/2 oz. lemon juice
1/2 oz. pineapple juice
Pineapple leaves

Half-fill a cocktail shaker with ice. Add the melon liqueur, Cointreau, vodka, lemon juice, and pineapple juice. Shake vigorously and strain into a chilled cocktail glass. Garnish with pineapple leaves.

diablo

No sand, no insects, no seaweed. This has to be better than the real thing!

sex on the beach

Ice cubes
1½ oz. vodka
½ oz. peach schnapps
1½ oz. pineapple juice
1½ oz. cranberry juice
Crushed ice

Half-fill a cocktail shaker with ice. Add the vodka, schnapps, pineapple juice, and cranberry juice and shake well. Strain into a tall cocktail glass half-filled with crushed ice.

When nothing else is quite as it seems, rest assured this fruity fantasy has nothing to hide.

masquerade

Ice cubes
1 1/2 oz. citrus vodka
1/2 oz. apple schnapps
1 oz. watermelon juice
1/2 oz. apple juice
Dash of lime juice
Thin apple slices

Half-fill a cocktail shaker with ice. Add the vodka, schnapps, watermelon juice, apple juice, and dash of lime juice. Shake vigorously and strain into a chilled martini glass. Garnish with thin slices of apple.

A capital drink capturing the balmy breezes, vibrant life, and vivid colors of Cuba.

Havana special

Ice cubes
2 oz. pineapple juice
1/3 oz. cherry brandy
1 1/2 oz. white rum
Stemmed cocktail cherry

Half-fill a cocktail shaker with ice. Add the pineapple juice, cherry brandy, and rum. Shake vigorously and strain into a cocktail glass half-filled with ice. Garnish with a stemmed cocktail cherry.

Mambo around the palm tree and let the rum help you rhumba like a red-hot mama.

Bahama mama

Ice cubes
1/2 oz. Malibu
1/2 oz. Kahlúa
1/2 oz. dark rum
1/2 oz. white rum

Crushed ice
Pineapple juice
Thin pineapple wedge
Mint sprig

Half-fill a cocktail shaker with ice. Add the Malibu, Kahlúa, and the dark and white rum. Shake vigorously, then strain into a highball glass half-filled with crushed ice. Top up with pineapple juice and garnish with a pineapple wedge and a sprig of mint on the rim.

masquerade

A fantasy island adventure in a tumbler.

Barbados fondue

Half a lime, chopped
Half a mango, peeled
6 small chunks of young coconut flesh
1/2 oz. sugar syrup
Ice cubes
1 1/2 oz. peach-infused vodka (see recipe on page 25)
1 oz. guava juice
Strawberry half

Muddle the lime, mango, and coconut with the sugar syrup in a cocktail shaker. Add a scoop of ice, then the vodka and guava juice. Shake vigorously, pour into a chilled tumbler, and garnish with half a strawberry.

A bountiful paradise in the palm of your hand—cocolossal!

coconut reef

6 small chunks of young coconut flesh
Half a lime, chopped
1/2 oz. sugar syrup
Ice cubes
11/2 oz. peach-infused vodka (see recipe on page 25)
1 oz. strawberry purée (see recipe on page 23)
Cranberry juice

Muddle the coconut and lime with the sugar syrup in a cocktail shaker. Add a scoop of ice, then the vodka and strawberry purée. Shake vigorously and strain into a tall glass 1 inch from the top, then top up with cranberry juice.

The tango requires passion, style, and coordination, so it's probably a good idea to dance first, drink later.

mango tango

1/2 oz. mango liqueur
1/2 oz. Grand Marnier
1/2 oz. sugar syrup
1/2 oz. cream
1/2 oz. milk
Half a mango, peeled and diced
8 ice cubes
Mango purée (see recipe on page 23)

Place the mango liqueur, Grand Marnier, sugar syrup, cream, milk, mango, and ice in a heavy-duty blender and blend until thick and smooth. Pour into a tall, chilled cocktail glass and garnish with a swirl of fresh mango purée.

Aren't we lucky the power-packed banana helps take the edge off the previous night's bender?

banana bender

Crushed ice
1/2 oz. Cointreau
1/2 oz. banana liqueur
2 oz. cream
Half a banana, sliced
Maraschino cherry

Place the crushed ice, Cointreau, banana liqueur, cream, and banana in a blender and blend well. Pour into a chilled champagne flute and garnish with a maraschino cherry.

Barbados fondue

It's easy to get spliced on this wondrous pine-melon fusion.

It can happen in a trice.

splice

1/2 cup crushed ice
1/2 oz. melon liqueur
1/2 oz. Cointreau
1/2 oz. Malibu
31/2 oz. pineapple juice
2 oz. cream
Pineapple wedge
Melon ball

Place the crushed ice, melon liqueur, Cointreau, Malibu, pineapple juice, and cream in a blender and blend well. Pour into a large, chilled goblet. Garnish with a wedge of pineapple and a melon ball. Serve with a straw.

Saint-Tropez is so very far from here, but with this chic number, a Riviera moment is just a swizzle stick away.

chichi

1/2 cup crushed ice
11/2 oz. vodka
1/2 oz. Malibu
1/2 oz. coconut cream
1/2 cup pineapple juice
Pineapple wedge
Strawberry slices

Place the crushed ice, vodka, Malibu, coconut cream, and pineapple juice in a blender and blend well. Pour into a large, chilled tumbler and garnish with a small wedge of pineapple and strawberry slices.

This really should be drunk out of a hollowed-out pineapple, and preferably in the shallow end of the pool!

piña colada

1 cup crushed ice
1 1/2 oz. white rum
1/2 oz. coconut cream
1/2 oz. Malibu
3 1/2 oz. pineapple juice
1/2 oz. sugar syrup
Pineapple leaves

Place the crushed ice, rum, coconut cream, Malibu, pineapple juice, and sugar syrup in a blender and blend until the consistency of shaved ice. Pour into a large, chilled cocktail glass and garnish with pineapple leaves and a cocktail umbrella.

Unfurl an umbrella, spread out a towel, purloin a couple of coconuts, and stake out your own little corner of the Caribbean.

coco colada

1 1/2 oz. brown crème de cacao
1/2 cup pineapple juice
1 1/2 oz. coconut cream
1/2 cup crushed ice
Pineapple wedge

Place the crème de cacao, pineapple juice, coconut cream, and the crushed ice in a blender and blend until smooth. Pour into a large, chilled cocktail glass and garnish with a pineapple wedge.

chichi

muddled   It isn't always such a bad thing to feel a little muddled. Indeed, a muddled cocktail is a wonderful thing! The drinks in this chapter draw their inspiration from exotic corners of the globe, seeking out wild combinations of delirious new flavors to baffle the tongue, awaken the taste buds, and send your senses spinning. It's only natural to feel a little disoriented. Follow your nose and you'll be fine . . .

It all began **innocently** enough, as excellent adventures often do. Someone **muddled** and mashed and ground and gently bashed some fruit and herbs around in a cocktail shaker, releasing a burst of powerfully fresh flavors into our tired old drinks, instantly firing up our fatigued palates. Suddenly we were bounding about in Chile—or was it Peru?—sampling copious amounts of **pisco**, a clear, brandylike spirit that both countries claim as their national drink. Who are we to argue? Next stop Brazil, where we took on board some **cachaça**, a sterling distillation of unrefined sugarcane juice roughly translating as "farmer's drink." But it was only when somebody muddled some kiwifruit and ginger into their **caipiroska** that things started getting really confusing! Sometime around sunset, we cruised off into the Caribbean for some crazy **mojitos**, then meandered down Mexico way to sample a little **gold tequila**, simultaneously stumbling upon some wondrous new tequilas spiked with vanilla, chili, and cinnamon! After our feisty, fiery Latino lovers, we happily surrendered to a strangely sweet Asian intrigue, seduced by wildly wonderful **vodkas** tasting of lemongrass, citrus, cinnamon, and honey, with a dash of mint-infused dry vermouth, and flavors crushed from citrus, cilantro, cucumber, **tamarillo**, blood orange, and **lemongrass**. Where we are now, nobody knows, but life will never be the same again.

235

Make like an ancient and celebrate the spirit of South America with the national drink of Chile and Peru.

pisco sour

Ice cubes
1/2 oz. lemon juice
1/3 oz. sugar syrup
1 1/2 oz. pisco
Maraschino cherry

Half-fill a cocktail shaker with ice. Add the lemon juice, sugar syrup, and pisco, then shake well. Strain into a chilled sour glass and garnish with a maraschino cherry.

Start your party with a round of Brazil's finest export and you'll Mardi Gras all the way to Rio.

caipirinha

1 lime, chopped
1 tablespoon superfine sugar
1/2 oz. sugar syrup
Ice cubes
2 oz. cachaça
Mint sprig

Muddle the lime with the sugar and sugar syrup in a cocktail shaker. Add a scoop of ice and the cachaça. Shake vigorously, strain into a chilled tumbler, and garnish with a sprig of mint.

A caipirinha made from vodka rather than cachaça. Boy, those Brazilians sure know how to create a carnival atmosphere!

caipiroska

1 lime, chopped
1 tablespoon superfine sugar
1/2 oz. sugar syrup
Ice cubes
2 oz. vodka

Muddle the lime with the sugar and sugar syrup in a cocktail shaker. Add a scoop of ice and the vodka. Shake vigorously and strain into a chilled tumbler.

BARTENDER'S TIP You could make a minty caipiroska by muddling eight mint leaves with the lime, sugar, and sugar syrup.

The vibrant flavors in this lively number will make your tongue do a capoeira and your body bossa nova!

kiwifruit and ginger caipiroska

1 kiwifruit, peeled
Half a lime, chopped
1 teaspoon superfine sugar
Ice cubes
1 1/2 oz. honey vodka
1/2 oz. ginger liqueur

Muddle the kiwifruit and lime with the sugar in a cocktail shaker. Add a scoop of ice, then the vodka and ginger liqueur. Shake vigorously and strain into a chilled tumbler.

BARTENDER'S TIP Honey vodka is commercially available, but if your liquor store can't supply it, substitute plain vodka.

caipiroska

This Cuban classic is sure to get your mojo going. But first a word of warning: they're supernaturally addictive!

mojito

8 mint leaves
Half a lime, chopped
1/2 oz. sugar syrup
Ice cubes
2 oz. white rum
Club soda

Muddle the mint and lime with the sugar syrup in a cocktail shaker. Add a scoop of ice, then the rum. Shake vigorously and strain into a chilled tumbler 1 inch from the top, then top up with club soda.

Cilantro in a cocktail? Sounds a little cuckoo, but try it once and you'll be stalking another.

cilantro mojito

1 handful cilantro
1 lime, chopped
1 teaspoon sugar
1/2 oz. sugar syrup
Ice cubes
2 oz. white rum
Club soda

Muddle the cilantro and lime with the sugar and sugar syrup in a cocktail shaker. Add a scoop of ice, then the rum. Shake vigorously and strain into a chilled tumbler 1 inch from the top, then top up with club soda.

The sparkling riches gleaming within may prove irresistibly alluring. Get out your shovel and start digging.

Acapulco gold

1 lemon, chopped
1/2 oz. sugar syrup
Ice cubes
1 1/2 oz. chili-infused tequila (see recipe on page 24)
1/2 oz. vanilla liqueur
Lemonade

Muddle the lemon and sugar syrup in a cocktail shaker. Add a scoop of ice, then the tequila and vanilla liqueur. Shake vigorously and strain into a tall, chilled glass 1 inch from the top, then top up with lemonade.

When the Latin rhythm starts to play, slurp, suck, or lick one of these and start to sway.

lambada lick

Half a peach, chopped
1 oz. passion fruit purée
1/2 oz. sugar syrup
Ice cubes
11/2 oz. cachaça
Dash of lime juice

Muddle the peach and passion fruit purée with the sugar syrup in a cocktail shaker. Add a scoop of ice, then the cachaça and lime juice. Shake vigorously and strain into a chilled tumbler.

Acapulco gold

Down Mexico way there's a lake called Chapala. Now if only there were a lake *made* of chapala . . .

chapala

5 small chunks of watermelon
1 lime, chopped
1/2 oz. sugar syrup
Ice cubes
1 1/2 oz. gold tequila
Apple juice

Muddle the watermelon and lime with the sugar syrup in a cocktail shaker. Add a scoop of ice, then the tequila. Shake vigorously and strain into a tall, chilled glass 1 inch from the top, then top up with apple juice.

If your day's been a disaster, you may as well go out with a bang and celebrate in style.

ginger fiasco

Ice cubes
1 1/2 oz. gold tequila
1/2 oz. ginger liqueur
1 oz. guava juice
1/3 oz. lime juice
1/2 oz. sugar syrup
1 pineapple leaf

Half-fill a cocktail shaker with ice. Add the tequila, ginger liqueur, guava juice, lime juice, and sugar syrup. Shake vigorously and strain into a chilled martini glass. Garnish with a pineapple leaf.

Destined to stir the passions of any hot-blooded woman.

señorita

1 1/2 tablespoons raspberries
1 1/2 tablespoons blueberries
1/2 oz. sugar syrup
Ice cubes
1 1/2 oz. gold tequila
1/2 oz. raspberry liqueur
1 oz. cranberry juice
Lime wedge

Muddle the raspberries and blueberries with the sugar syrup in a cocktail shaker. Add a scoop of ice, then the tequila and raspberry liqueur. Shake vigorously and strain into a chilled tumbler 1 inch from the top, then top up with cranberry juice. Garnish with a wedge of lime.

Will bring even the proudest man to his knees.

el hombre

Half a lemon, chopped
1 oz. peach purée (see recipe on page 23)
1/2 oz. sugar syrup
Ice cubes
11/2 oz. vanilla-infused tequila (see recipe on page 25)
1/2 oz. peach liqueur

Muddle the lemon and peach purée with the sugar syrup in a cocktail shaker. Add a scoop of ice, then the tequila and peach liqueur. Shake vigorously and strain into a chilled tumbler.

señorita

Whip one of these out of your cape whenever you need a flash of panache or a shot of brazen courage.

matador

Ice cubes
1 1/2 oz. cinnamon-infused tequila (see recipe on page 24)
1/2 oz. apple schnapps
1/2 oz. lemon juice
1 oz. apple juice
1/2 oz. sugar syrup
Thin apple slice

Half-fill a cocktail shaker with ice. Add the tequila, apple schnapps, lemon juice, apple juice, and sugar syrup. Shake vigorously and strain into a chilled martini glass. Garnish with a slice of apple.

Love makes the world go round, but matchmakers make the love go round.

matchmaker

1 tamarillo, chopped
8 mint leaves
$1/2$ oz. sugar syrup
Ice cubes
$11/2$ oz. honey vodka
$1/2$ oz. cinnamon-infused vodka (see recipe on page 24)
$1/3$ oz. lime juice
Orange twist

Muddle the tamarillo and mint with the sugar syrup in a cocktail shaker. Add a scoop of ice, then the two vodkas and lime juice. Shake vigorously and strain into a chilled martini glass. Garnish with a twist of orange.

To enjoy a blood sunset in all its glory can be a rather intoxicating experience.

blood sunset

3 strawberries, halved
Half a blood orange, chopped
1/2 oz. sugar syrup
Ice cubes
1 1/2 oz. vodka
Dash of lime juice

Muddle the strawberries and blood orange with the sugar syrup in a cocktail shaker. Add a scoop of ice, then the vodka and lime juice. Shake vigorously and pour into a chilled tumbler.

Jump into your zaniest costume and you'll really start to dig this outlandishly colorful outfit.

zoot suit

Half an orange, chopped
Half a lime, chopped
1/2 oz. sugar syrup
Ice cubes
1 1/2 oz. Campari
1 oz. blood-orange juice

Muddle the orange and lime with the sugar syrup in a cocktail shaker. Add a scoop of ice, then the Campari and blood-orange juice. Shake vigorously and strain into a chilled tumbler.

zoot suit

For a crash course in Eastern philosophy, meditate on this.

lemongrass martini

Ice cubes
2 oz. lemongrass-infused vodka (see recipe on page 24)
1/2 oz. ginger liqueur
1/2 oz. sugar syrup
1 Kaffir lime leaf or lime twist

Half-fill a cocktail shaker with ice. Add the vodka, ginger liqueur, and sugar syrup. Shake vigorously and strain into a chilled martini glass. Garnish with a lime leaf or twist of lime.

Forget flower power—try some grassroots sour power!

lemongrass sour

Ice cubes
1¹/2 oz. lemongrass-infused vodka (see recipe on page 24)
¹/2 oz. Cointreau
¹/2 oz. sugar syrup
1 oz. ruby-red grapefruit juice
1 small stem of lemongrass

Half-fill a cocktail shaker with ice. Add the vodka, Cointreau, sugar syrup, and grapefruit juice. Shake vigorously and strain into a chilled martini glass. Garnish with a stem of lemongrass.

The coolest drink in the world just got cooler.

mint and cucumber martini

8 cucumber slices
10 mint leaves
1/3 oz. sugar syrup
Ice cubes
2 1/3 oz. gin
1/3 oz. mint-infused dry vermouth (see recipe on page 24)
2 cucumber batons

Muddle the cucumber and mint with the sugar syrup in a cocktail shaker. Add a scoop of ice, then the gin. Coat the inside of a chilled martini glass with the vermouth. Place a small sieve over the martini glass and strain the martini into the glass. (This is known as "double straining," which ensures a lovely, clear drink.) Garnish with two cucumber batons.

Slap on a Carmen Miranda hat and your brightest bright-red lipstick and let the showgirl in you shimmy.

Lindy Lopez

4 chunks of pineapple
Half a lemon, chopped
1/2 oz. sugar syrup
Ice cubes
1 1/2 oz. citrus vodka
1/2 oz. vanilla liqueur

Muddle the pineapple and lemon with the sugar syrup in a cocktail shaker. Add a scoop of ice, then the vodka and vanilla liqueur. Shake vigorously and strain into a chilled tumbler.

mint and cucumber martini

club lounge   After a long, hard day spent engaged in strictly masculine pursuits, it was customary for men of good breeding to unwind in the rarefied ambience of the nineteenth hole, otherwise known as the gentleman's bar. In this world away from women, the

man about town was free to indulge in a little dignified swilling of a

clutch of classic drinks. All in good fun. Who could blame them?

Stake your place on a dark leather chesterfield and sink down into a man's own world where topics of great importance and jocularity are mulled over at leisure, tall tales are traded, and deals are done over a card game and a drink or three. Settle back as the shadows lengthen from late in the afternoon until deep into the evening. Perhaps Sir would care to begin with a few afternoon refreshments, a sundowner, or an appetite-provoking aperitif? We venture to suggest Sir might also wish to sample some classics mixed from gin and vodka, or perhaps some relaxing brandy-based drinks, or if Sir has had a very rugged day, he might prefer to proceed directly to our straight talkin', sharp shootin', hard-hitting, no-nonsense types such as whiskey or bourbon. And when the business of the day is done, Sir may wish to sample a little snifter of late-night, top-shelf liqueurs such as cognac, Drambuie, and Bénédictine. A word to the wise bar manager: invest in some Pimm's No. 1, Campari, amaretto, and vermouth; stock up on lemon, orange, grapefruit, and tomato juices and mixers such as club soda, ginger ale, and lemonade; and check your supply of bitters, Tabasco, Worcestershire, lime juice cordial, grenadine, and sugar syrup. Naturally, garnishes are free of feminizing influences: a maraschino cherry is as fancy as it gets, but the usual adornments are slices of lemon, orange, or cucumber. Remember, discretion is the key . . .

A British institution, Pimm's No. 1 is the commercial version of a gin sling, traditionally taken after a spot of tennis or golf.

Pimm's

Ice cubes
1½ oz. Pimm's No. 1
Lemonade
Ginger ale
Slice of cucumber skin
Orange slice
Lemon slice

Half-fill a highball glass with ice. Add the Pimm's, then top up with lemonade and ginger ale. Garnish with slices of cucumber skin, orange, and lemon.

In the Prohibition years, the Americano was freely enjoyed as a "medicinal" compound. James Bond was also partial to a few.

Americano

Ice cubes
1/2 oz. Campari
1/2 oz. sweet vermouth
Club soda
Orange slice
Lemon slice

Half-fill an old-fashioned glass with ice. Add the Campari and vermouth, then top up with club soda. Garnish with slices of orange and lemon and serve with a swizzle stick.

Invented more than a century ago in a London restaurant named Pimm's, this old classic slings you back into another age.

gin sling

Ice cubes
1½ oz. gin
½ oz. lemon juice
Dash of grenadine (optional)
⅓ oz. sugar syrup
Club soda

Half-fill an old-fashioned glass with ice. Add the gin, lemon juice, grenadine, and sugar syrup, then top up with club soda. Garnish with a cocktail umbrella.

Created around the eve of World War I, this is the drink that made Singapore's Raffles Hotel famous.

Singapore sling

Ice cubes	1 oz. orange juice
1½ oz. gin	1 oz. pineapple juice
½ oz. Bénédictine	Dash of lime juice
½ oz. Cointreau	Dash of grenadine
½ oz. cherry brandy	Maraschino cherry

Half-fill a cocktail shaker with ice. Add all the ingredients except for the garnish, then shake well and strain into a tall glass half-filled with ice. Garnish with a maraschino cherry.

Singapore sling

Steel your resolve and face the world with a gimlet eye.

At the very least, you'll ward off scurvy.

gimlet

Ice cubes
1½ oz. gin
½ oz. lime juice
½ oz. lime juice cordial
Lime twist
Lime wedge

Half-fill a mixing glass with ice. Add the gin, lime juice, and lime juice cordial and stir well. Strain into a chilled goblet and garnish with a twist of lime and a wedge of lime.

Those spirited old sailors of the high seas knew full well not to go overboard on lime rickeys.

lime rickey

Ice cubes
1 1/2 oz. gin
1/2 oz. sugar syrup
1/2 oz. lime juice
Dash of Angostura bitters
Club soda
Lime twist
Lime slice

Half-fill a highball glass with ice. Add the gin, sugar syrup, lime juice, and a dash of bitters, then top up with club soda. Garnish with a twist of lime and a slice of lime.

So many places and people lay claim to inventing the
Tom Collins, one of the great stayers of cocktail history.

Tom Collins

Ice cubes
1¹/2 oz. gin
1 oz. lemon juice
¹/2 oz. sugar syrup
Club soda
Stemmed cocktail cherry

Half-fill a highball glass with ice. Add the gin, lemon juice, and sugar syrup.
Stir well and top up with club soda. Garnish with a cocktail cherry.

Tall tales are easy to tell with a couple of salty dogs under your belt. Just remember to let sleeping dogs lie.

salty dog

Lemon wedge
Salt
Ice cubes
1 1/2 oz. vodka
Grapefruit juice
Lime wedge

Wipe the wedge of lemon around the rim of an old-fashioned glass, then dip the rim in a saucer of salt, shaking off any excess. Fill the glass with ice three-quarters full, add the vodka, and then top up with grapefruit juice. Garnish with a wedge of lime.

gimlet

Traditionally used as the "hair of the dog," this invigorating tonic is too good to save for the morning after.

Bloody Mary

3 ice cubes

1½ oz. vodka

4 drops of Tabasco sauce

1 teaspoon Worcestershire sauce

⅓ oz. lemon juice

Pinch of salt

1 grind of black pepper

2 oz. chilled tomato juice

1 crisp celery stalk

Place the ice cubes in a highball glass, pour in the vodka, and then add the Tabasco, Worcestershire sauce, and lemon juice. Add the salt and pepper, then pour in the tomato juice and stir well. Allow to sit for a minute, then garnish with a stalk of celery.

BARTENDER'S TIP For extra zing, you could garnish your Bloody Mary with wedges of lemon and lime.

Swing out, sister, and travel in style—just remember to pack your goggles, because it might be a bumpy ride.

sidecar

Ice cubes
1 oz. brandy
1/2 oz. Cointreau
1 oz. lemon juice
Lemon twist

Half-fill a cocktail shaker with ice. Add the brandy, Cointreau, and lemon juice, then shake well. Strain into a chilled cocktail glass and garnish with a twist of lemon.

Everyone should have one of these in his or her toolbox.

screwdriver

Ice cubes
1½ oz. vodka
Orange juice
Maraschino cherry
Orange twist

Three-quarters fill a highball glass with ice. Add the vodka and top up with orange juice. Garnish with a maraschino cherry and a twist of orange and serve with a straw.

Only warm familiarity and years of shared memories can take you down this long and winding road.

slow comfortable screw

Ice cubes
1/2 oz. vodka
1/2 oz. gin
1/2 oz. Southern Comfort
Orange juice
Orange twist

Fill a highball glass with ice three-quarters full. Add the vodka, gin, and Southern Comfort. Stir, top up with orange juice, and garnish with a twist of orange.

Bloody Mary

A classy beverage, but not for high tea. Just remember, one is a potent social lubricant, two will knock you off your feet.

Long Island iced tea

Ice cubes
1/2 oz. white rum
1/2 oz. vodka
1/2 oz. gin
1/2 oz. Cointreau
1/2 oz. tequila
1/2 teaspoon lime juice
Cola
Lime wedge

Half-fill a highball glass with ice. Add the rum, vodka, gin, Cointreau, tequila, and lime juice, then top up with cola. Stir well with a swizzle stick and garnish with a wedge of lime.

After a long, hot, and sultry day, here's something tall, cool, and soothing to settle your sulky Southern belle.

mint julep

Ice cubes
2 oz. bourbon
8 mint leaves
1/2 oz. sugar syrup
Dash of dark rum or brandy
Mint sprig

Half-fill a mixing glass with ice. Add the bourbon, mint, and sugar, then stir. Strain into a highball glass filled with ice and stir gently until the glass becomes frosted. Top with a dash of rum or brandy. Garnish with a sprig of mint and serve with a long straw.

BARTENDER'S TIP Some people add a few chunks of cucumber for extra refreshment.

It tastes of almond, but amaretto (Italian for "a little bitter") is derived from apricot pits. Doesn't that drive you nuts?

amaretto sour

Ice cubes
1 oz. amaretto
1 oz. lemon juice
1/2 oz. orange juice
Maraschino cherry

Half-fill a cocktail shaker with ice. Add the amaretto, lemon juice, and orange juice and shake well. Strain into a chilled sour glass and garnish with a maraschino cherry.

Misery loves company, so if you're feeling a little taciturn, spend some time with a strong, silent type.

brandy sour

Ice cubes
1 oz. brandy
1 oz. lemon juice
1/2 oz. sugar syrup
Maraschino cherry

Half-fill a cocktail shaker with ice. Add the brandy, lemon juice, and sugar syrup, strain into a chilled sour glass, and garnish with a maraschino cherry.

mint julep

Glittering brightly like an amber ambrosia, this shining libation will help you find your sparkle.

brandy, lime, and soda

Ice cubes
1 oz. brandy
Dash of lime juice cordial
1/2 oz. lime juice
Club soda
Lime twist

Half-fill an old-fashioned tumbler with ice. Add the brandy, lime juice cordial, and lime juice. Top up with club soda and garnish with a twist of lime.

Sometimes life is a bumpy ride. All you can do is cling tightly to the horse's neck and hope for the best.

horse's neck

Ice cubes
1¹/₂ oz. brandy
1 teaspoon Angostura bitters
Ginger ale
1 lemon, for the "horse's head"

Fill a highball glass with ice. Add the brandy, then the bitters. Top with ginger ale and garnish with a horse's head.

BARTENDER'S TIP To make a horse's head garnish, carefully peel away the skin of a lemon in one long piece. Tie a knot in one end. Drape the knotted end over the inside edge of the highball glass, leaving most of the peel dangling outside the glass.

Slow down, Sonny, pull up a chair, linger awhile, and reflect on days gone by.

old-fashioned

1 sugar cube
Dash of Angostura bitters
Club soda
Ice cubes
2 oz. bourbon
Orange twist (optional)

Place the sugar cube in an old-fashioned glass. Add the bitters and let it soak into the sugar. Add a splash of club soda and enough ice to half-fill the glass. Pour in the bourbon and stir to dissolve the sugar. Garnish with a twist of orange, if desired.

Whether you want to get high or just have a ball, this drink lives up to its name.

highball

Ice cubes
1 1/2 oz. rye whiskey
Club soda or ginger ale
Lemon twist

Half-fill a highball glass with ice. Add the whiskey and top up with club soda or ginger ale. Garnish with a twist of lemon.

old-fashioned

Take a little walk on the wry side and spend some time with a smart-talking Manhattan.

Manhattan dry

Ice cubes
2 oz. rye whiskey
1/2 oz. dry vermouth
Dash of Angostura bitters
Orange twist

Half-fill a cocktail shaker with ice. Add the whiskey, vermouth, and bitters, then shake well. Strain into a chilled cocktail glass and garnish with a twist of orange.

Cities don't come bigger than the Big Apple, and drinks don't come classier than this.

New Yorker

Ice cubes
1½ oz. rye whiskey
1 teaspoon lime juice
Dash of grenadine
Orange twist

Half-fill a cocktail shaker with ice. Add the whiskey, lime juice, and grenadine. Shake well, strain into a cocktail glass, and garnish with a twist of orange.

There's nothing quite like a brisk tumbler in the rye.

whiskey sour

Ice cubes
1 1/2 oz. rye whiskey
1/2 oz. Cointreau
1/2 oz. lemon juice
1/2 oz. sugar syrup
Maraschino cherry

Half-fill a cocktail shaker with ice. Add the whiskey, Cointreau, lemon juice, and sugar syrup, and shake well. Strain into a tumbler and garnish with a maraschino cherry.

For a brave, brave heart, slip a few under your kilt.

Rob Roy

Ice cubes
2 oz. Scotch whisky
1 oz. sweet red vermouth
Dash of Angostura bitters
Maraschino cherry

Half-fill a cocktail shaker with ice. Add the whisky, vermouth, and bitters, then shake well. Strain into a chilled cocktail glass and garnish with a maraschino cherry.

New Yorker

A supremely powerful entity demanding the utmost respect.

godfather

Ice cubes
1¹/2 oz. Scotch whisky
¹/2 oz. amaretto

Fill an old-fashioned glass with ice, then pour the whisky and amaretto in the glass.

Who needs a magic wand when you have one of these?

godmother

Ice cubes
1 1/2 oz. vodka
1/2 oz. amaretto

Fill an old-fashioned glass with ice, then poor the vodka and amaretto in the glass.

Dark, mysterious, and complex—just like every good romance.

French connection

Ice cubes
1/2 oz. cognac
1/2 oz. amaretto

Half-fill an old-fashioned glass with ice. Add the cognac, then the amaretto. Stir well.

Hit the nail on the head with this hammer of a drink.

rusty nail

Ice cubes
1½ oz. Scotch whisky
1½ oz. Drambuie
Half an orange slice

Half-fill an old-fashioned tumbler with ice. Add the whisky and Drambuie, then garnish with half a slice of orange.

Hallelujah to those saintly monks whose mystical ministrations gave rise to this accommodating potion.

B & B

1/2 oz. brandy
1/2 oz. Bénédictine

Pour the brandy and Bénédictine into a warmed brandy balloon. Gently swill the liquid around the glass, take a good sniff of its fiery contents, and then sip slowly.

Say hello to an exotic stranger who is as dark as night and just as intriguing.

black Russian

Ice cubes
1¹/₂ oz. vodka
1 oz. Kahlúa

Half-fill an old-fashioned glass with ice. Add the vodka and Kahlúa and stir.

rusty nail

mellow Creamy, milky, sweet, and dreamy, these cocktails are surely sent from high above to melt away the cares of the mortal day. At the end of a meal, these mellifluous offerings are like manna from heaven, delivering to all good people their just deserts, radiating smiles of deep

contentment and a warm inner glow. Soothing and sublime, they are

the supreme indulgence. Go on, you *know* you want to . . .

This chapter has special meaning for people who are blessed with a pronounced predilection for creamy concoctions infused with sugar and spice and all things nice. This is the chapter where liqueurs are in their element, where heaven meets earth, and angels sing high up in the firmament (you might need to sip a few liqueurs to hear them). The word "liqueur" derives from the Latin meaning "to melt," or "to dissolve"—a very accurate description of their mellowing effects upon the human body. Liqueurs have been around for centuries and it seems they are now available in every conceivable flavor from fruity and herbal to coffee and chocolate. Just as well, really. And while they can be combined in innumerable ways, the liqueurs you'll find cropping up in the most popular of our mellow cocktails include Frangelico, Irish cream, Cointreau, Grand Marnier, Galliano, Tia Maria, Kahlúa, chocolate liqueur, advocaat, and crème de cacao, and divine fruit liqueurs such as strawberry, melon, and raspberry. Which is not to say you have to buy them all to be the consummate host—but then again, who's to stop you? Other valued friends from the spirit world that make their influence keenly felt here include gin, vodka, and brandy, with special dispensation given to indulge in milk, cream, chocolate syrup, chocolate, freshly grated nutmeg, crushed hazelnuts, coffee, cloves, and cinnamon. Why delay? Life is short!

Who was Alexander? Who cares? But could somebody pour the man a drink?

brandy Alexander

Ice cubes
1 oz. brandy
1/2 oz. brown crème de cacao
1 oz. cream
Freshly grated nutmeg

Half-fill a cocktail shaker with ice. Add the brandy, crème de cacao, and cream, and shake vigorously. Strain into a chilled cocktail glass and dust with nutmeg sprinkled over two crossed straws.

No need to bother with dinner. A bowl of this will fill you up and warm the cockles of your heart.

eggnog punch

5 eggs, separated
1 1/3 cups sugar
1 cup bourbon
1 cup cream
3/4 cup milk
Freshly grated nutmeg

Whisk the egg whites until stiff, then slowly add a third of the sugar, whisking constantly until glossy. In a large serving bowl, beat the egg yolks with a third of the sugar until the sugar has dissolved. Slowly add the bourbon, whisking well. In another bowl, lightly whisk the cream with the remaining sugar until the sugar has dissolved. Gently fold the egg whites into the yolk mix, then fold in the cream. Slowly stir in the milk, then chill for 4 hours. Serve each glass dusted with a little grated nutmeg. Serves 10.

Frankly, my dear, after several of these you certainly will not give a damn.

Frankie

Ice cubes
½ oz. Frangelico
½ oz. Kahlúa
1 oz. Irish cream
1 oz. cream
Very finely crushed hazelnuts

Half-fill a cocktail shaker with ice. Add the Frangelico, Kahlúa, Irish cream, and cream. Shake vigorously, then strain into a large chilled cocktail glass. Serve sprinkled with very finely crushed hazelnuts.

Sometimes comfort is the order of the day. Let this fluffy favorite unruffle your feathers and smooth away your troubles.

fluffy duck

Ice cubes
1/2 oz. advocaat
1/2 oz. gin
1/2 oz. Cointreau
1 oz. orange juice
1 oz. cream
Lemonade

Half-fill a highball glass with ice. Add the advocaat, gin, Cointreau, orange juice, and cream, then top up with lemonade.

Frankie

Our darkly mysterious acquaintance, the black Russian,

suddenly takes on a creamy complexion.

white Russian

Ice cubes
1 oz. vodka
1 oz. Kahlúa
1/2 oz. cream

Half-fill an old-fashioned glass with ice. Add the vodka and Kahlúa, then carefully float the cream on top by pouring it over the back of a teaspoon.

They have ways to make you talk—tell them nothing you'll regret in the morning.

KGB

1/2 oz. Kahlúa
1/2 oz. Irish cream
1/2 oz. Grand Marnier

Pour the Kahlúa into a shot glass, then carefully float the Irish cream on top by pouring it over the back of a teaspoon. Using a clean teaspoon, float the Grand Marnier over the Irish cream so you have three distinct layers.

Clear the bar, line 'em up, and bombs away, baby.

B-52

1/2 oz. Kahlúa
1/2 oz. Irish cream
1/2 oz. Cointreau

Pour the Kahlúa into a shot glass, then carefully float the Irish cream on top by pouring it over the back of a teaspoon. Using a clean teaspoon, float the Cointreau over the Irish cream so that you have three distinct layers.

No harm in setting the scene for a ravishing encounter.

seduction

1/2 oz. Kahlúa
1/2 oz. melon liqueur
1/2 oz. Irish cream

Pour the Kahlúa into a shot glass, then carefully float the melon liqueur on top by pouring it over the back of a teaspoon. Using a clean teaspoon, float the Irish cream over the melon liqueur so that you have three distinct layers.

B-52

Stake your place in the summer sun and drift away on a cloud of dreams.

golden dream

Ice cubes	1 oz. orange juice
1/2 oz. Galliano	1 oz. cream
1/2 oz. Cointreau	Orange twist

Half-fill a cocktail shaker with ice. Add the Galliano, Cointreau, orange juice, and cream. Shake vigorously and strain into a large, chilled cocktail glass. Garnish with a twist of orange.

When two heavenly ingredients come together, the result can only be bliss.

strawberries and cream

Egg white
Superfine sugar
1/2 oz. strawberry liqueur
1/2 oz. Tia Maria
1/2 oz. Irish cream

1 oz. cream
3 ripe strawberries
1 cup crushed ice
Strawberries

Dip the rim of a cocktail glass in a saucer of egg white, then a saucer of sugar, shaking off any excess. Chill. Pour the strawberry liqueur, Tia Maria, Irish cream, and cream into a blender. Add the strawberries and blend until smooth, then add the ice and blend until the mixture is the consistency of shaved ice. Pour into the sugar-frosted cocktail glass and garnish with strawberries on a cocktail skewer.

A sinfully wicked cocktail to be slurped with slow abandon.

cherry ripe

Ice cubes
1½ oz. Frangelico
1 oz. raspberry liqueur
1 oz. lime juice
Maraschino cherry

Half-fill a cocktail shaker with ice. Add the Frangelico, raspberry liqueur, and lime juice, then shake vigorously and strain into a chilled martini glass. Garnish with a maraschino cherry.

Has a habit of ganging up on you, in the nicest possible way.

malt mafia

3 tablespoons raspberries
1/3 oz. sugar syrup
Ice cubes
1 1/2 oz. chocolate malt vodka
1 oz. vanilla liqueur
Fresh raspberries

333

Muddle the raspberries with the sugar syrup in a cocktail shaker. Add a scoop of ice, then the vodka and vanilla liqueur. Shake vigorously and strain into a chilled tumbler. Garnish with fresh raspberries.

malt mafia

Keep reminding yourself, this is *not* a chocolate milk shake.

Toblerone

1 teaspoon honey
1/2 oz. chocolate syrup
Finely chopped hazelnuts
Ice cubes
1/2 oz. Frangelico

1/2 oz. Irish cream
1/2 oz. Tia Maria
1/2 oz. creamy chocolate liqueur
2 oz. cream
Shaved chocolate

Drizzle the honey and a teaspoon of the chocolate syrup into a large chilled martini glass. Sprinkle with chopped hazelnuts and chill. Half-fill a cocktail shaker with ice. Pour in the Frangelico, Irish cream, Tia Maria, chocolate liqueur, and cream and shake well. Strain into the chilled martini glass and garnish with shaved chocolate.

A chocolate martini! Are we in heaven yet?

chocotini

⅓ cup roughly chopped chocolate
Ice cubes
2 oz. vodka
1 oz. brown crème de cacao

Melt the chocolate in a heatproof bowl over simmering water. Dip the rim of a martini glass in the chocolate, or dot the chocolate around the rim. Chill the glass. Half-fill a cocktail shaker with ice. Add the vodka and crème de cacao, shake vigorously, and strain into the chilled martini glass.

You've been so good—gone for a salad, passed on the dessert—but whoops, you've slipped up big time now.

mudslide

1/3 cup roughly chopped dark chocolate
Ice cubes
1/2 oz. Kahlúa
1 1/2 oz. Irish cream
1/2 oz. vodka

Melt the chocolate in a heatproof bowl over simmering water. Dip the rim of an old-fashioned glass in the melted chocolate, then half-fill the glass with ice. Add the Kahlúa, Irish cream, and vodka and stir.

A little indulgence is a wonderful thing, but two cups of it are better than one.

amaretto liqueur coffee

2/3 cup roughly chopped dark chocolate, melted
2 oz. amaretto
2 1/2 cups hot, strong espresso coffee
1/2 cup cream
2/3 oz. pure maple syrup
1/3 cup Vienna almonds, roughly chopped

Coat two spoons with the melted chocolate and leave on a saucer in the fridge for about an hour to set. Divide the amaretto between two coffee glasses and pour in the coffee. Whisk the cream until stiff peaks form, then fold in the maple syrup. Spoon a dollop of cream into each coffee glass and sprinkle with the chopped almonds. Serve with the chocolate spoons. Serves 2.

chocotini

Too many of these cute little critters might very well give you the jitters.

coffee Jell-O shots

2 oz. hot coffee
3/4 teaspoon powdered gelatin
3 oz. Tia Maria
1/3 oz. sugar syrup
Whipped cream
Grated chocolate

Mix 1 tablespoon of the hot coffee with the gelatin until smooth, then stir into the remaining coffee until the gelatin is dissolved. Allow to cool, then add the Tia Maria and sugar syrup. Pour into six shot glasses and refrigerate for 3 hours, or until set. Before serving, top with a dollop of whipped cream and sprinkle with grated chocolate. Makes 6.

Claim some sanity from the lunar madness and there'll be howls of thanks all around.

full moon

Ice cubes
1/2 oz. white rum
1/2 oz. Kahlúa
1 teaspoon sugar
Pinch of ground cloves
Pinch of ground cinnamon
2/3 cup cold espresso
1/2 oz. cream

Three-quarters fill a highball glass with ice. Add the rum, Kahlúa, and sugar and stir well until the sugar has dissolved. Add the cloves and cinnamon, then top up with the coffee. Float the cream over the top by carefully pouring it over the back of a teaspoon.

It may take a few shots to get this right. Then have another shot using butterscotch schnapps instead of the Sambuca.

that's the shot

2 oz. Sambuca
2 oz. Kahlúa
Coffee beans

Divide the Sambuca between two shot glasses. Carefully float the Kahlúa on top by pouring it over the back of a teaspoon so you have two distinct layers. Float a few coffee beans on top. Serves 2.

We all love our creature comforts, so when you're onto a good thing, milk it to the hilt.

brown cow

Ice cubes
1 oz. Tia Maria
2 oz. milk
Ground cinnamon

Half-fill a cocktail shaker with ice. Add the Tia Maria and milk, shake vigorously, and strain into a chilled cocktail glass. Sprinkle with cinnamon.

full moon

A nightcap to give any budding romance a blooming chance.

caramel bud

Ice cubes
1/2 oz. butterscotch schnapps
1 oz. chocolate liqueur
1/2 oz. white crème de cacao
1 oz. cream
Grated chocolate

Half-fill a cocktail shaker with ice. Add the butterscotch schnapps, chocolate liqueur, crème de cacao, and cream. Shake vigorously and strain into a chilled cocktail glass. Garnish with grated chocolate.

Sheer luxury! Why wear anything else?

silk stocking

Ice cubes
1/2 oz. butterscotch schnapps
1/2 oz. advocaat
1 oz. white crème de cacao
1 oz. cream
White chocolate shards

Half-fill a cocktail shaker with ice. Add the butterscotch schnapps, advocaat, crème de cacao, and cream. Shake vigorously and strain into a chilled martini glass. Garnish with shards of white chocolate.

A creamy concoction kissed with coffee, whisky, oranges, and chocolate. What's not to love?

orange moon

Ice cubes
1/2 oz. Kahlúa
1/2 oz. Scotch whisky
1/2 oz. Grand Marnier
1 oz. orange juice
1/2 oz. cream
Shaved chocolate curls
Orange twist

Half-fill a cocktail shaker with ice. Add the Kahlúa, whisky, Grand Marnier, orange juice, and cream. Shake vigorously and strain into a chilled cocktail glass. Garnish with shaved chocolate curls and a twist of orange.

A cunning diversion to bring the rowdy elements under control. Works like clockwork every time.

chocwork orange

Ice cubes
1 oz. chocolate liqueur
1/2 oz. Kahlúa
1/2 oz. Grand Marnier
1 oz. cream
Orange-flavored chocolates

Half-fill a cocktail shaker with ice. Add the chocolate liqueur, Kahlúa, Grand Marnier, and cream. Shake vigorously and strain into a chilled cocktail glass. Before serving, drop a few chocolates into the glass.

silk stocking

Settle back, sink down, and stretch those legs out. It's time for some seriously smooth cruising.

golden Cadillac

Ice cubes
1 oz. Galliano
1 oz. white crème de cacao
1 oz. cream

Half-fill a cocktail shaker with ice. Add the Galliano, crème de cacao, and cream. Shake vigorously, then strain into a chilled cocktail glass.

It looks harmless enough, but this enticing creature comes with a nip in its tail.

stinger

Ice cubes or crushed ice
1 1/2 oz. brandy
1/2 oz. white crème de menthe
Maraschino cherry

Place some ice cubes or crushed ice in a small highball glass. Add the brandy and crème de menthe and stir well. Garnish with a maraschino cherry.

One of these and you'll be begging for another, and then another, and another . . .

orgasm

Ice cubes
¹/₂ oz. Cointreau
¹/₂ oz. Irish cream
Strawberry
2 cherries

Half-fill an old-fashioned glass with ice. Add the Cointreau and Irish cream and stir. Garnish with a strawberry and two cherries.

Oh honey, if it's got you screaming, you just know it must be good for you.

screaming orgasm

Ice cubes
1/2 oz. Galliano
1/2 oz. Irish cream
1/2 oz. Cointreau
1/2 oz. Kahlúa
1 oz. cream
Strawberry

Half-fill a cocktail shaker with ice. Add the Galliano, Irish cream, Cointreau, Kahlúa, and cream, then shake vigorously. Strain into a chilled martini glass and garnish with a strawberry.

stinger

A delicate drink that will bring a fresh, petal-like blush to your cheeks.

apple blossom

Ice cubes
1 oz. apple schnapps
1 oz. vodka
1/2 oz. white crème de cacao
1/2 oz. cream
Freshly grated nutmeg

Half-fill a cocktail shaker with ice. Add the apple schnapps, vodka, crème de cacao, and cream, then shake vigorously. Strain into a chilled cocktail glass and sprinkle with grated nutmeg.

Crack out the fondue set—the seventies are back and this joint is hopping.

grasshopper

Ice cubes
1/2 oz. green crème de menthe
1/2 oz. white crème de cacao
2 oz. cream
Grated chocolate

Half-fill a cocktail shaker with ice. Add the crème de menthe, crème de cacao, and cream. Shake vigorously and strain into a chilled martini glass. Garnish with grated chocolate.

Raise a toast to the Ottoman empire and dream of glories lost.

Turkish martini

Ice cubes
1 1/2 oz. vanilla vodka
1 oz. white crème de cacao
1/3 oz. rose water
Small cube of Turkish delight

Add a scoop of ice to a cocktail shaker, then the vodka, crème de cacao, and rose water. Shake vigorously and strain into a chilled martini glass. Garnish with a cube of Turkish delight.

Musky, dusky, and deeply exotic—a princely offering indeed.

maharaja

2 cardamon pods
1/2 oz. sugar syrup
Ice cubes
11/2 oz. vodka
1 oz. dark crème de cacao
Mint sprig

Pound the cardamon pods with the sugar syrup in a cocktail shaker. Add a scoop of ice, then the vodka and crème de cacao. Shake vigorously and strain into a chilled martini glass. Garnish with a sprig of mint.

Turkish martini

After raising a racket all evening, this champion serve is just the ace you need to complete the grand slam.

Wimbledon

Ice cubes
1¹/2 oz. vanilla vodka
¹/2 oz. white crème de cacao
¹/2 oz. strawberry liqueur
1 oz. milk
1 teaspoon shaved dark chocolate

Add a scoop of ice to a cocktail shaker, then the vodka, crème de cacao, strawberry liqueur, and milk. Shake vigorously, strain into a chilled martini glass, and sprinkle with shaved chocolate.

Break into one of these before buzzing off to bed and it'll bee sweet dreams all the way.

honeycomb

Ice cubes
1 1/2 oz. honey vodka
1 1/2 oz. vanilla vodka
1/2 oz. sugar syrup
2 vanilla beans

Add a scoop of ice to a cocktail shaker, then the two vodkas and the sugar syrup. Shake vigorously and strain into a chilled martini glass. Garnish with two vanilla beans.

BARTENDER'S TIP Honey vodka is commercially available but can be hard to obtain. If you can't find it, use extra vanilla vodka, which is more commonly available, or infuse your own (see recipe on page 25).

Vanilla was once highly prized as an aphrodisiac. This silky-smooth martini is a lovely tonic indeed.

vanilla martini

Ice cubes
2 oz. vanilla vodka
1/2 oz. Grand Marnier
1/2 oz. sugar syrup
Vanilla bean

Add a scoop of ice to a cocktail shaker, then the vodka, Grand Marnier, and sugar syrup. Shake vigorously and strain into a chilled martini glass. Garnish with a vanilla bean.

All aboard this glorious contrivance of perky coffee and dreamy vanilla.

vanilla express

Ice cubes
1 oz. gold tequila
1 oz. vanilla vodka
1 oz. chilled espresso coffee
1/2 oz. sugar syrup
5 coffee beans

Add a scoop of ice to a cocktail shaker, then the tequila, vodka, coffee, and sugar syrup. Shake vigorously and strain into a tumbler. Sprinkle the coffee beans over the top.

honeycomb

A powerful home remedy for dirty, rotten head colds. A cup before retiring and you won't feel a thing.

hot toddy

4 teaspoons brown sugar
4 slices of lemon
4 cinnamon sticks
12 whole cloves
1/2 cup Scotch whisky
4 cups boiling water

Put all the ingredients in a heatproof container. Stir, leave for a few minutes, then strain. Serve in heatproof glasses. Serves 4.

Ahoy there! Here's a rummy old trick to beat off the ills and chills of deepest, darkest winter.

buttered rum

4 teaspoons sugar
1 cup rum
2 cups boiling water
Softened unsalted butter

Place the sugar, rum, and boiling water in a heatproof pitcher. Stir to dissolve the sugar, then divide among four mugs. Stir 1–2 teaspoons of butter into each mug and enjoy hot. Serves 4.

Use the very best port you can lay your hands on for this curiously complex drink.

porto flip

Ice cubes
1 oz. brandy
1 1/2 oz. red port
Egg yolk
Freshly grated nutmeg

Half-fill a cocktail shaker with ice. Add the brandy, port, and egg yolk, then shake vigorously. Strain into a cocktail glass and sprinkle with nutmeg.

Ponder the mysteries of the heavens above with this saintly blend of red, red wine and earthy spices.

monks' spiced mulled wine

1 orange
12 cloves
4 tablespoons brown sugar
1 whole nutmeg, grated
3 cinnamon sticks
2 lemons, sliced
1 bottle dry red wine

Stud the orange with the cloves and place in a large saucepan. Add the sugar, nutmeg, cinnamon sticks, lemon slices, and 2 cups water. Stir over low heat until the sugar has dissolved. Bring to a boil, reduce the heat, and simmer for 15 minutes. Add the red wine and heat through. Serves 4–6.

porto flip

virginal Sometimes it's perfectly acceptable to fake it—for instance, when you have a headache from having had a little too much the evening before, or if you really must keep your wits about you. Sitting soft has never been such an appealing option with this memorable collection of marvelous mocktails. So there's really no reason why nondrinkers can't come to the party and have a smashing good time!

In these enlightened times, we all know one must never drink and drive, so when a designated driver turns up on your doorstep with a gaggle of misfits intent on serious mischief, as a dutiful host it is incumbent on you to ensure our civic-minded friend isn't left entirely high and dry or at least empty handed! Of course, it isn't only drivers who need subtle diversions from inebriating pursuits. There are in our population certain abstemious types, as well as those unruly, undisciplined souls who turn up at a party nursing rather dastardly hangovers and yet who can't quite manage to stay away! Thankfully, there are far more interesting creations than just boring soft drinks or a tired old glass of tap water in which sits a sad squelch of lemon to offer. Some of the spectacularly innocent mocktails gathered herein look just like the real thing, without the sting, so your nondrinking guests will arise with sparkling clear heads the next morning—unlike you, poor thing. Some you'll want to drink just for the sheer taste of it. What follows is a fine sprinkling of bubbly brews and luscious slushes, effervescent spiders and fizzes, caffeinated creations for a quick kick-start, and creamy delights you could really enjoy any time of day. A great proportion of these mocktails are also astonishingly rejuvenating and bursting with nutrients—so don't be too surprised if you stumble upon a certain hangover remedy or two . . .

Surely one of the few true virgins on the party circuit.

Virgin Mary

Lemon wedge
2 teaspoons celery salt
1 teaspoon black pepper
Ice cubes
1/2 cup tomato juice
1/2 oz. lemon juice
1 teaspoon Worcestershire sauce
Dash of Tabasco sauce
Celery stalk

Wipe the lemon wedge around the rim of a large goblet, then dip the rim in the combined celery salt and pepper. Half-fill a cocktail shaker with ice. Add the tomato juice, lemon juice, Worcestershire, and Tabasco sauce and shake well. Strain into the frosted goblet and garnish with a celery stalk.

Open the hatches, hold the nose, and, shucks, down she goes.

prairie oyster

1/2 oz. Worcestershire sauce
2 drops Tabasco sauce
Egg yolk
Good dash of salt and pepper

Combine the Worcestershire and Tabasco sauce in an old-fashioned glass.
Gently slide in the egg yolk, taking care to keep it intact. Season with salt
and pepper, then swallow in one gulp.

Cinderella scrubbed the floor and slept in the hearth but won a waistline to die for—oh, and a handsome prince.

Cinderella

1 1/2 oz. orange juice
1 1/2 oz. pineapple juice
1/2 oz. lemon juice
Ice cubes

Pour the orange juice, pineapple juice, and lemon juice into a cocktail shaker. Add a scoop of ice, shake vigorously, then strain into a chilled martini glass.

Bring a dimple to the cheeks of whoever's steering the good ship lollipop home tonight.

Shirley Temple

Ice cubes
Good dash of grenadine
Ginger ale or lemonade
1 oz. cream
Maraschino cherries

Place some ice in a tall glass, add the grenadine, and top with ginger ale or lemonade. Float the cream on top over the back of a teaspoon. Garnish with maraschino cherries and serve with a straw and a swizzle stick.

Cinderella

Party time for temperate taste buds.

mixed berry and pineapple frappé

2 cups fresh or frozen mixed berries
1 1/3 cups chopped pineapple
1 cup pineapple juice
1/2 teaspoon rose water
6–8 ice cubes, crushed

Place the berries, pineapple, pineapple juice, rose water, and ice in a blender and blend until smooth. Pour into two tall chilled glasses. Serves 2.

A little tart with a nutty heart.

hazelnut sour

Ice cubes
3/4 oz. hazelnut syrup
2/3 oz. lime juice
3/4 cup club soda

Place some ice in a medium glass. Add the hazelnut syrup and lime juice, then stir in the club soda.

Almost as good as the real thing!

zing and tonic

Ice cubes
1/2 oz. ginger syrup/cordial
1/2 oz. lemon juice
Dash of Angostura bitters
3/4 cup tonic water

Place some ice in a medium glass. Add the ginger syrup, lemon juice, and a dash of bitters, then stir in the tonic water.

An excellent remedy when you're a little hot under the collar.

coolio

Half a small orange, peeled and finely diced
6 mint leaves
1/2 teaspoon superfine sugar
3/4 cup club soda

Muddle the orange and mint leaves with the sugar in a wide-mouthed, medium glass. Top up with the club soda.

mixed berry and pineapple frappé

An edgy lemonade for sober-minded sophisticates.

blueberry swoon

Ice cubes
1/2 cup blueberry juice
1/2 oz. lemon juice
1/2 cup lemonade

Place some ice in a medium glass. Add the blueberry juice and lemon juice, then stir in the lemonade.

A drink of the vine that won't thrash the head.

grape bash

10 seedless black grapes
Half a small lime, chopped
½ cup sparkling grape juice

Muddle the grapes and lime in a tall glass until pulpy, then top up with the grape juice.

It looks a little murky, but it'll smooth over any storm.

pulp friction

1 1/2 oz. lime juice
1 teaspoon superfine sugar
1 teaspoon tamarind concentrate
4 large ice cubes
1/2 cup lemonade

Place the lime juice, sugar, tamarind concentrate, and ice cubes in a heavy-duty blender and blend until smooth. Pour into a medium glass and top up with the lemonade.

An exquisite antidote to the sting of summer.

watermelon and rose water slush

2 cups frozen watermelon chunks
1½ oz. lime juice
1 teaspoon rose water

Place the frozen watermelon, lime juice, and rose water in a blender and blend until smooth. Pour into a tall glass.

grape bash

Give tired taste buds the razzle-dazzle treatment.

sweet tang

1 cup strawberries or raspberries
1/2 cup cranberry juice

Place the berries and cranberry juice in a blender and blend until smooth.
Pour into a medium glass.

BARTENDER'S TIP If fresh berries aren't in season, use frozen instead.

A citrus sling with a ring of sweetness.

lemonade

Egg white
Superfine sugar
Juice of 1 lemon
Juice of 1 lime
Club soda
Sugar syrup

Dip the rim of two medium glasses in a saucer of egg white, then a saucer of sugar, shaking off any excess. Chill the glasses. Mix the lemon juice and lime juice together in a pitcher. Pour into the sugar-frosted glasses, then top up with club soda. Stir in sugar syrup to taste. Serves two.

Brew up a batch and wait for the sparks to fly.

passion brew

1/2 cup guava juice
Pulp of 1 small passion fruit
3 mint leaves, very finely chopped
3 large ice cubes
2¾ oz. sparkling grapefruit drink

Place the guava juice, passion fruit pulp, mint, and ice in a cocktail shaker. Shake vigorously, pour into a medium glass, and top up with the sparkling grapefruit drink.

First impressions are deceiving—she's sweeter than she looks.

feisty redhead

12 raspberries
Half a small lime, chopped
1 1/2 teaspoons pomegranate syrup
1/2 teaspoon superfine sugar
2/3 cup ginger beer

Muddle the raspberries and lime with the pomegranate syrup and sugar
in a wide-mouthed medium glass until pulpy. Top up with the ginger beer.

lemonade

The buzz about town is that this sparkling potion is fit to pop.

kiwifruit–apple cider fizz

2 kiwifruits, peeled and finely sliced
Juice of 1 lime
3 cups nonalcoholic sparkling apple cider

Divide the kiwifruit slices between two glasses. Combine the lime juice and apple cider and pour over the kiwifruit. Serves 2.

Guaranteed to keep you cool, calm, and collected.

spice island tea

1 tea bag (such as English breakfast)
Large pinch of ground cinnamon
Small pinch of ground allspice
1 cup boiling water
Ice cubes
1/2 oz. lemon juice
1/2 cup ginger ale
Lemon slice

Place the tea bag and spices in a mug and pour in the boiling water. Allow to cool, then refrigerate until well chilled. Pour the spiced tea into a large, tall glass over ice, then add the lemon juice and ginger ale. Garnish with a slice of lemon.

A tropical daydream that won't send you loco.

troppococo

Half a small mango, peeled and chopped
2/3 cup pink grapefruit juice
2 oz. coconut milk
2 teaspoons superfine sugar
3 large ice cubes

Place the mango, grapefruit juice, coconut milk, sugar, and ice in a heavy-duty blender and blend until smooth. Pour into a medium glass.

Enjoy by the pool or in the pool, any time of the day.

piña coolada

1/2 cup coconut milk
1/2 cup pineapple juice
5 large ice cubes

Place all the ingredients in a heavy-duty blender and blend until smooth.
Pour into a tall glass.

troppococo

Makes you feel all warm and gooey.

smooch

1 large scoop chocolate ice cream
2 teaspoons hazelnut syrup
3 teaspoons chocolate syrup
2 teaspoons malted milk powder
1/2 cup milk
3 chocolate-coated malt candies, crushed

Place the ice cream, hazelnut syrup, chocolate syrup, malt powder, and milk in a blender and blend until smooth. Pour into a medium glass and garnish with crushed malt candy.

Don't hold back, make a song and dance about it!

espress yourself

1/2 cup espresso coffee, chilled
1 teaspoon honey
A few drops pure vanilla extract
Pinch of ground cinnamon
2 3/4 oz. cream
3 large ice cubes
Extra honey, for drizzling

Place the espresso, honey, vanilla extract, cinnamon, cream, and ice cubes
in a heavy-duty blender and blend until smooth. Pour into a medium glass
and drizzle with a little extra honey.

An entertaining, all-American classic.

Mickey Mouse

Ice cubes
Cola
1 scoop vanilla ice cream
Whipped cream
3 maraschino cherries

Place some ice in a tall glass. Add enough cola to fill the glass two-thirds full, then float a scoop of ice cream on top and top with some whipped cream. Garnish with maraschino cherries.

A bittersweet reminder of all those happy days.

cherry cola

Ice cubes
1/2 cup vanilla-flavored cola
1/2 cup sour cherry juice
Maraschino cherry, with stem

Place some ice cubes in a tall glass. Combine the cola and cherry juice and pour into the glass. Garnish with a maraschino cherry.

A beautiful drink that does wonders for the complexion.

blushing peach

½ cup peach juice
½ cup almond milk
Good dash of Angostura bitters
Ice cubes
Drizzle of grenadine

Combine the peach juice, almond milk, and bitters in a cocktail shaker with five large cubes of ice. Shake well, then strain into a medium glass. Drizzle with a little grenadine and use the tip of a knife to gently swirl the grenadine into a pretty pattern.

So simple, so yummy, who needs dessert?

eggnog

1 egg
1/2 teaspoon pure vanilla extract
2 teaspoons superfine sugar
1/2 cup cream
1/2 cup milk
Large pinch freshly grated nutmeg, plus extra for sprinkling
3 large ice cubes

Crack the egg into a heavy-duty blender and add the vanilla, sugar, cream, milk, nutmeg, and ice cubes. Blend until smooth and frothy. Pour into a medium glass and sprinkle with a little extra grated nutmeg.

blushing peach

glossary

advocaat creamy brandy-based Dutch liqueur made with egg yolks, sugar, and vanilla.

amaretto a lush yet slightly bitter almond-flavored Italian liqueur.

Angostura bitters an aromatic infusion of herbs and spices, now made in Trinidad but originally devised as a medicinal tonic by an army doctor in Angostura, Venezuela.

aperitif a drink taken before a meal under the pretext of stimulating the appetite.

aperol dark-orange Italian aperitif distilled from herbs and roots such as gentian, rhubarb, and bitter orange. It has a sweet orange taste.

Bénédictine brandy-based French liqueur spiced with dozens of herbs, invented in 1510 by a Benedictine monk.

bourbon a corn-mash whiskey originating in Bourbon County, Kentucky.

brandy fiery amber spirit distilled from grapes and aged in oak, which takes its name from the Dutch word for "burned wine." It can be flavored with other fruits such as cherry, plum, and peach.

cachaça (ka-shah-sah) clear Brazilian spirit distilled from unrefined sugarcane juice, with a burned sugar taste.

Calvados an apple brandy produced only in the French region of Normandy.

Campari pungent, ruby-red Italian bitters laced with herbs and quinine.

Chartreuse French liqueur flavored with over 130 herbs and spices, originally created by old Carthusian monks as a medicinal elixir. The green version is more pungent than the yellow.

Cognac fine brandy made from a grape variety grown only around the French province of Cognac.

Cointreau clear, brandy-based French liqueur laced with the peel of sweet and bitter Spanish and Caribbean oranges.

crème de cacao liqueur tasting of vanilla and roasted cocoa beans, available white (clear) or brown.

crème de menthe sweet liqueur flavored with mint and spearmint, available in two varieties: white (clear) or bright green.

curaçao orange-flavored, spirit-based liqueur available in many colors. It is named after the Caribbean island where the dried, bitter orange peel traditionally used in its manufacture was sourced.

digestif any drink taken after dinner, be it mixed or creamy. Digestifs are reputed to aid the digestion.

Drambuie liqueur blended from fine aged Scotch whiskys, herbs, and spices.

Frangelico toasted hazelnut liqueur produced in the Piedmont region of northern Italy.

gin this clear spirit, also known as "mother's ruin" and "Dutch courage," made from grain and flavored with juniper berries and other botanicals was developed by a Dutch doctor in 1650.

Galliano sweet, yellow Italian liqueur flavored with herbs, flowers, and spices, with a distinct anise flavor.

Grand Marnier a luscious Cognac flavored with the peel of bitter Haitian oranges and spices such as vanilla.

grenadine nonalcoholic, bright-red cordial, used to add color and sweetness to cocktails.

Kahlúa dark Mexican liqueur with a toasted coffee flavor.

lime juice cordial thick syrup made from concentrated lime juice and sugar.

limoncello sweet Italian aperitif flavored with huge, juicy lemons grown around Sorrento and the Amalfi coast.

Mandarine Napoleon fine Belgian Cognac-based liqueur infused with essential oils of Sicilian tangerines and various herbs.

Parfait Amour lilac-colored French liqueur flavored with herbs and citrus.

Pernod clear French aniseed-flavored spirit.

Pimm's Pimm's No. 1 is the commercial version of a gin sling, sweetened with spices, fruits, and herbs. Pimm's No. 2 is brandy-based.

pisco clear, fiery brandy distilled from white grapes, named after a port in Peru, and also from the large clay pots in which the grapes were traditionally fermented.

Poire William luscious French brandy distilled from the Bartlett pear.

rum synonymous with sailors, rebellions, pirates, and the tropics, this popular spirit is distilled from sugarcane juice or molasses and can be clear, brown, or almost black.

sake Japanese rice wine.

Sambuca anise-flavored Italian liqueur infused with the witch elder bush and white elder blossoms. The clear version is more widely used, but a stronger-tasting black version is also available.

schnapps generic term for a spirit distilled from grain or potato, often flavored with fruits or herbs. The infusion can be dry, like vodka, or very sweet and liqueurlike (such as peach and butterscotch schnapps).

sugar syrup boiling sugar and water produces a syrup that's easier to mix into drinks than crystallized sugar. Buy it prepared or make it yourself (see recipe on page 23).

Tia Maria dark liqueur made from Jamaican Blue Mountain coffee beans.

tequila named after a small town in Mexico, this fiery spirit takes its flavor from the heart of the blue agave, a succulent member of the lily family. It is made only in three states in Mexico. Gold tequila is aged in wooden barrels for several months, imparting a subtle amber hue.

vermouth fortified white-wine aperitif flavored with aromatic roots, herbs, spices, and fruit peels, derived from the German word for "wormwood." Dry vermouth is pale, and also known as French vermouth. Sweet vermouth may be white (bianco) or red (rosso) and is also referred to as Italian vermouth.

vodka Russian for "dear little water," this versatile spirit looks and tastes almost like water. A huge range of infused vodkas are now available (see the recipes on pages 24–25). Smooth operators keep theirs in the freezer.

whiskey, whisky Celtic for "water of life"! Scottish malt whisky is made from spring water and malted barley smoked over a peat fire, matured in oak barrels. Irish whiskey also uses malted barley, but without the smoking process. Canadian whiskey, often called rye whiskey, is made from rye and other grains such as corn, wheat, and barley.

423

drink finder

Looking for your favorite tipple? The cocktails in this drink finder are listed alphabetically, as well as by their dominant base spirit (or spirits) and style of drink. So if you're hankering for a brandy-based drink, have a look under "brandy." If you're in need of a martini, look up "martini." If you know the name of the cocktail, you will find it in the alphabetical index. The cocktails are categorized according to the following base liqueurs and spirits: amaretto, bourbon, brandy, cachaça, Campari, champagne and wine, gin, Pimm's, pisco, rum, sake, tequila, vodka, and whiskey. The drinks are also listed according to the following styles: coladas, daiquiris, digestifs, eggnogs and flips, fizzes and spritzers, Jell-O shots, margaritas, martinis, mocktails, punches, and sours. Happy hunting!

426

427

429

alphabetical index

430

431